CONTENTS

THE PREQUEL TRILOGY

STAR WARS™

COLLECTOR'S EDITION 2013

Pedigree®

Published 2012. Pedigree Books Ltd, Beech Hill House,
Walnut Gardens, Exeter, Devon EX4 4DH
books@pedigreegroup.co.uk   www.pedigreebooks.com

A long time ago in a galaxy far, far away....

It's 35 years since *Star Wars* first launched upon the world and we were introduced to the Jedi, the Force and the infamous Darth Vader. The *Star Wars Collector's Edition 2013* takes you to the beginning of the saga of Anakin Skywalker, delving deep into the stories of *Star Wars:* Episodes I, II and III alongside hundreds of fantastic images from the amazing films.

While Darth Sidious plots to divide and conquer the galaxy, the Jedi attempt to maintain peace against ever-growing threats. Anakin, who might be the one prophesied to bring balance to the Force, faces the trials of becoming a Jedi and confronts the fears that pull him toward the dark side. From the discovery of Anakin on Tatooine and Qui-Gon Jinn's meeting with the fearsome Darth Maul to the outbreak of the Clone Wars and the rise of the Empire, the *Star Wars Collector's Edition 2013* charts one of the most tumultuous times in the history of the galaxy.

Also featured are in-depth profiles on the most important people, creatures and droids from the *Star Wars* prequels, and surprising facts about some of the most beloved characters. So prepare to venture into a universe of intrigue, war, incredible planets, alien creatures and an epic battle between good and evil....

STAR WARS™
EPISODE I
THE PHANTOM MENACE™

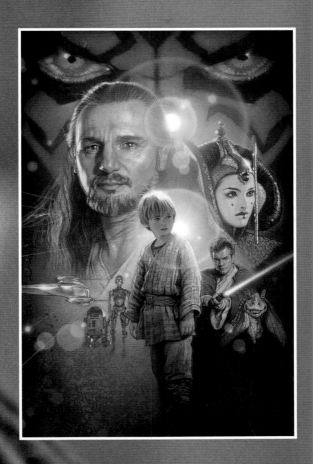

Turmoil has engulfed the Galactic Republic. The taxation of trade routes to outlying star systems is in dispute.

Hoping to resolve the matter with a blockade of deadly battleships, the greedy Trade Federation has stopped all shipping to the small planet of Naboo.

While the congress of the Republic endlessly debates this alarming chain of events, the Supreme Chancellor has secretly dispatched two Jedi Knights, the guardians of peace and justice in the galaxy, to settle the conflict....

ANAKIN SKYWALKER

Born a slave on Tatooine, Anakin Skywalker seems to have only a life of servitude ahead of him. The arrival of Jedi warriors Qui-Gon Jinn and Obi-Wan Kenobi changes his existence completely. Qui-Gon immediately senses Anakin's strong connection to the Force and believes the boy may be the long-prophesied Chosen One who will bring balance to the Force.

At nine-years-old, Anakin is considered too old to start training to become a Jedi. The Jedi Council also worries that his clouded future, as well as the fear and anger they sense within him, make him unfit to become a member of the Order. Qui-Gon nevertheless keeps Anakin close by in order to guide the boy's journey to adulthood. After Qui-Gon's death at the hand of Darth Maul, the Jedi Council agrees to allow Obi-Wan to take Anakin as his Padawan.

As a young man, Anakin begins to strain against the strictures of Jedi life. Obi-Wan teaches restraint and control, but Anakin has trouble keeping his emotions in check. He even bends the Jedi Code and forms a romantic attachment to the beautiful Senator Padmé Amidala, whom he eventually marries.

When Anakin discovers his mother has been taken by Tusken Raiders, he attempts to save her but arrives too late and she dies. This and his desire to protect Padmé sets him off him off on a path towards the dark side. Chancellor Palpatine urges Anakin to give in to his anger, eventually revealing his secret identity as Darth Sidious to the impressionable young Jedi. Anakin, enticed by power and acting from fear, completes his descent to the dark side and takes on the Sith identity of Darth Vader.

DID YOU KNOW?

When we meet Anakin Skywalker in the films, he is owned by the junk dealer Watto. Earlier in his life he was the property of crime lord Gardulla the Hutt. Gardulla had a major gambling habit and ended up losing Anakin and his mother, Shmi Skywalker, in a Podracing bet.

OBI-WAN KENOBI

Born on the planet Stewjon, Obi-Wan Kenobi showed Jedi promise from an early age and was taken as the apprentice of Qui-Gon Jinn. Towards the end of his Jedi training, Obi-Wan begins to play a pivotal role in the fate of the galaxy, when he and Qui-Gon encounter the young Anakin Skywalker.

A powerful and shrewd fighter, he is the first Jedi in over a thousand years to defeat a Sith Lord when he battles Darth Maul. In the aftermath of the fight, Obi-Wan becomes a Jedi Master and is permitted to take Anakin as his Padawan. Obi-Wan can be tenacious when faced with a mystery, such as when he learns that a planet called Kamino seems to be missing from the Jedi archive. His investigation into this leads him to the discovery of a clone army, supposedly built at the behest of the Jedi, and the revelati on that a major shift in galactic powers is in the works.

Obi-Wan is known as a skilled negotiator who uses his dry wit to break tension and can stay calm in any situation. He recognises Anakin's strengths and weaknesses and tries to guide his sometimes reckless Padawan. But even he is unable to keep his apprentice from falling to the dark side. When the Republic has fallen, Obi-Wan stows away on Padmé's ship in the hope she will lead him to her husband. This takes him to the volcanic planet of Mustafar and an epic confrontation between the Jedi Master and his former apprentice unfolds. After nearly defeating Vader, Obi-Wan is unable to bring himself to finish off his former Padawan. He leaves him to die, which allows the Emperor to arrive and rescue Vader's broken body.

DID YOU KNOW?

Obi-Wan's homeworld, Stewjon, was officially announced by George Lucas at the Celebration V convention in 2010. The planet's name is a play on US talk show host/comedian Jon Stewart, who was interviewing Lucas at the event.

QUI-GON JINN

Renowned as one of the most powerful and clever Jedi Masters, Qui-Gon Jinn also has a reputation as a bit of a maverick. He is unafraid to chart his own path even if it skirts the wishes of the Jedi Council. Indeed it's his slightly rebellious attitude that keeps him from being on the Council himself. He's very much a man who lives for the moment and who believes that feeling the Force and trusting one's instincts are vital – a practice that he passes down to his apprentice, Obi-Wan Kenobi.

Qui-Gon may be known as a nonconformist, but he is still incredibly well respected both inside the Jedi Order and without. Wise, noble and compassionate, he has helped keep the peace and settle disputes on many worlds. The Jedi Master has had many challenges though, such as his Padawan Xanatos, who rebelled against Jedi Orders and ended up fighting against Qui-Gon in a civil war on Xanatos' homeworld of Telos. Qui-Gon is powerfully connected to the Force, allowing him to quickly realise that Anakin Skywalker may be the prophesied Chosen One and therefore someone who needs Jedi guidance.

Soon after Qui-Gon finds Anakin, he travels to the war-torn planet of Naboo, where he confronts the Sith Lord Darth Maul. Although Qui-Gon is renowned as one of the greatest masters of the lightsaber, Maul strikes a fatal blow to the Jedi. Even with his dying breath, Qui-Gon is more concerned with others than himself, asking Obi-Wan to train Anakin, a request Kenobi accepts.

DID YOU KNOW?

Count Dooku, who becomes Sith Lord Darth Tyranus and plays a critical role in the formation of the Galactic Empire, was Qui-Gon's Jedi Master when he was a Padawan.

JAR JAR BINKS

A Gungan from the planet Naboo, Jar Jar Binks was orphaned when his parents' habitat bubble was destroyed by a marauding sea monster. He is always keen to prove his worth, but his clumsiness causes him to live on the edge of his race's underwater society. After infuriating Gungan leader Boss Nass, he is exiled, which unexpectedly becomes the road to his redemption.

On Naboo's surface he literally bumps into Qui-Gon Jinn and Obi-Wan Kenobi. At their request, he helps the Jedi escape from the Trade Federation army by taking them to the Gungan stronghold of Otoh Gunga. Thanks to his playing an essential part in the Battle of Naboo and bringing a new understanding between the Gungans and the Naboo, Boss Nass decides Jar Jar must be a great warrior and makes him a general in the Gungan army. This ensures Jar Jar becomes one of the planet's most prominent citizens, and as a result he takes on the role of Senior Representative of Naboo alongside Senator Padmé Amidala in the Galactic Senate. Jar Jar may be derided by some in the Senate for his lack of acumen, but he is a rare example of a non-corrupt politician.

With the Separatist Alliance threatening war, initially Jar Jar favours negotiation and peaceful resolution over the growing popularity of the Military Creation Act. Unfortunately Jar Jar isn't the cleverest of politicians, so when Amidala leaves Coruscant and the Gungan takes her place in the Senate, he decides the situation has become so desperate that he puts forward a motion to grant Supreme Chancellor Palpatine the emergency powers needed to create a Grand Army of the Republic. This gives the future Emperor many of the tools he needs to take absolute control.

DID YOU KNOW?

Jar Jar Binks was exiled from the Gungan city of Otoh Gunga after he destroyed Boss Nass's gasser oven and then crashed the Gungan leader's luxury vehicle, known as a heyblibber.

A long time ago in a galaxy far, far away...

The Galactic Republic was in turmoil. Hoping to force Queen Amidala of Naboo to sign an unfavourable trade agreement, the greedy Trade Federation had stopped all shipping to Naboo by surrounding the planet with a blockade of deadly battleships.

While the Galactic Senate debated this alarming chain of events, the Supreme Chancellor Valorum secretly dispatched two Jedi – guardians of peace and justice in the galaxy – to settle the conflict.

In the cockpit of a Republic spacecruiser, Jedi Qui-Gon Jinn and his Padawan learner Obi-Wan Kenobi watched gravely as their craft hurtled towards one of the battleships forming the blockade.

The captain's view screen flickered to life and the image of Nute Gunray, Neimoidian Trade Viceroy, appeared.

"With all due respect for the Trade Federation, the ambassadors for the Supreme Chancellor wish to board immediately," the captain announced.

"Yes, yes, of course. As you know, our blockade is perfectly legal, and we'd be happy to receive the ambassadors." the Viceroy replied.

The screen went blank as the space cruiser prepared to dock inside the formidable battleship.

"I have a bad feeling about this," said Obi-Wan, he and Qui-Gon were escorted onto the ship by a protocol droid who took them into a conference room to await the Viceroy.

"I don't sense anything," replied the ever-calm Qui-Gon.

"It's not about the mission Master, it's something elsewhere... elusive," said Obi-Wan.

"Keep your concentration here and now where it belongs," warned Qui-Gon.

"Master Yoda says I should be mindful of the future," said Obi-Wan. "But not at the expense of the moment,' replied Qui-Gon. Be mindful of the living

Force, my young Padawan."

"How do you think this Trade Viceroy will deal with the Chancellor's demands?" asked Obi-Wan.

"These Federation types are cowards. The negotiations will be short," Qui-Gon assured his anxious apprentice.

Up on the bridge of the battleship, Viceroy Nute Gunray and his sidekicks Daultay Dofine and Rune Haako listened in stunned silence as the droid reported that the visitors were in fact Jedi.

"I knew it! They were sent to force a settlement. We're done for!" cried Dofine.

"Stay calm!" ordered Nute. "I'll wager the Senate isn't aware of the Supreme Chancellor's moves here.

Go! Distract them until I can contact Lord Sidious."

But Dofine did not move. "Are you brain dead? I'm not going in there with two Jedi," he puffed. "Send the droid!"

"I sense an unusual amount of fear for something as trivial as a trade dispute," Qui-Gon told Obi-Wan as they waited in the conference room.

The Jedi were becoming suspicious and rightfully so. Up on the bridge a mysterious, robed figure was at that very moment appearing by hologram. It was Darth Sidious.

"This scheme of yours has failed, Lord Sidious. The blockade is finished! We dare not go against these Jedi," squeaked Dofine.

Enraged by Dofine's impudence, Sidious dismissed him as "stunted slime" and called forward the Viceroy.

"This turn of events is unfortunate," he told Nute. "We must accelerate our plans, Viceroy. Begin landing your troops."

"My Lord, is that legal?" Nute quaked, fearful of Republic comeback should he invade Naboo.

"I will make it legal," roared Sidious.

"And the Jedi?" Nute asked.

"The Chancellor should never have brought them into this. Kill them immediately," came the order.

Suddenly an enormous explosion rocked the room. The Viceroy's guns had blasted the Republic space cruiser and crew into a million pieces.

Qui-Gon and Obi-Wan barely had time to draw their lightsabers and hold their breath before the conference room filled with gas.

"They must be dead by now," Nute's hologram told a squadron of battle droids gathered outside the conference room.

The door swished opened and it looked as if the Jedi were finished. Then, without warning, two flashing lightsabers flew out of the deadly fog, cutting down several battle droids.

As Nute and his crew looked on in horror, Qui-Gon and Obi-Wan continued their onslaught.

"Seal off the bridge. I want the destroyer droids up here. Close the blast doors!" Nute ordered frantically, as his crew cowered on the bridge.

But Nute had underestimated the power of a Jedi weapon.

Chunks of molten metal began to drop away as Qui-Gon's lightsaber stabbed through the doors to the bridge. He had almost broken through when…

"Destroyer droids!" yelled Qui-Gon, sensing their presence down the hallway.

He withdrew his lightsaber and turned with Obi-Wan to face the latest danger.

"I'd say this mission is past the negotiation stage," said Obi-Wan as the pair deflected the droids' blasts.

But the droids had shield generators and although the Jedi could defend themselves, they couldn't attack.

"It's a stand-off! Let's go!" shouted Qui-Gon and before the destroyers could react the crafty pair escaped up a nearby ventilation shaft.

Reaching the hanger bay they crouched in the shadows and watched thousands of battle droids loading onto landing craft.

At once the Trade Federation's true intentions became clear.

"An invasion army," exclaimed Obi-Wan.

"We've got to warn the Naboo and Chancellor

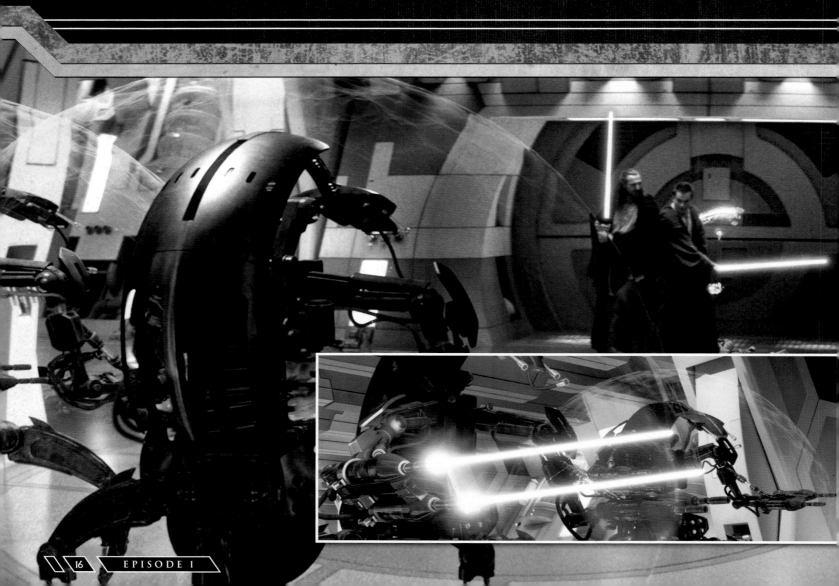

alorum," replied Qui-Gon.

The Jedi agreed to stow aboard ships bound or Naboo. "You were right about one thing, Master," smiled Obi-Wan. The negotiations were short!"

On the bridge, Nute's anxiety about the whereabouts of the wayward Jedi was temporarily forgotten as the image of Queen Amidala of Naboo flickered onto his view screen.

"At last we're getting results," Nute smirked to Rune before turning and addressing the Queen. "Again you come before me, Your Highness. The Federation is pleased."

"You will not be so pleased when you hear what I have to say, Viceroy. Your trade boycott of our planet has ended," Amidala answered.

"I was not aware of such a failure," said Nute

"Enough of this pretense, Viceroy!" snapped Amidala. "I'm aware the Chancellor's ambassadors are with you now and that you have been commanded to reach a settlement."

But to the Queen's surprise the Viceroy denied all knowledge of the Jedi ambassadors, telling her they would never act without the approval of the Senate.

As she signed off, he ordered his crew to disrupt all communications on Naboo to ensure the secrecy of the impending attack.

In her throne room on Naboo, the Queen, surrounded by her counsellors and handmaidens, discussed the situation with a hologram of Senator Palpatine of the Republic.

As Palpatine began to explain that the ambassadors had arrived to negotiate, the hologram sputtered and faded.

"A communications disruption can only mean one thing, Your Highness - invasion," cried Governor Bibble. "We must prepare to defend ourselves."

But Amidala was determined to negotiate for as long as possible.

"I will not condone a course of action that will lead us to war," she told her council.

The wise Queen may have favoured peace, but the Federation had other ideas: At that very moment their invasion force was arriving undetected on Naboo.

Six massive landing craft landed in the eerie swamp which covered one side of the planet. Huge troop transports began to roll out and head towards the cities.

A hologram of Nute appeared to the droid commander.

"There is no trace of the Jedi here. They may have gotten onto one of your landing craft," the Viceroy said.

"If they are down here, sir, we'll find them," replied the droid commander.

In another part of the swamp, Qui-Gon was running at full pelt through the misty marshes.

He glanced back to see the monstrous troop transports gaining on him. On every side panicked animals crashed out of the undergrowth, fleeing before the machines. But one creature seemed oblivious of the impending catastrophe. An odd, frog-like being – a Gungan named Jar Jar Binks – was crossing the swamp on the hunt for food.

Suddenly, he looked up to see Qui-Gon and the herd of creatures swarming towards him, followed by a huge troop transport.

"Help me!" he croaked, grabbing on to Qui-Gon, who dropped to the floor.

The war machine passed inches over their heads as they lay side by side in the mud.

"I luv yous," exclaimed Jar Jar, kissing Qui-Gon.

"Are you brainless?" cried the Jedi. "You almost got us killed!" Qui-Gon began to walk away, but his new friend was not easily shaken off.

"Mesa stay Mesa yous humble servant," said Jar Jar, telling Qui-Gon that, since he had saved his life, Jar Jar owed him a life debt.

As the pair moved through the swamp they met up with Obi-Wan and came under droid fire once more.

They needed to take cover – and fast!

"Ex-squeeze-me," Jar Jar piped up, "but da moto grande safe place would be Gunga City. Tis where I grew up."

The Gungan then had second thoughts, explaining he'd been banished. But when Obi-Wan explained the alternative was to stay and be blasted into oblivion by the invaders, Jar Jar agreed to lead them to the underwater city.

Using breathing masks plucked from their utility belts, Qui-Gon and Obi-Wan waded into the lake behind Jar Jar and swam into its murky depths.

Soon they saw the glow of Gunga City. Jar Jar showed them how to swim through one of the bubble membranes protecting the city from outsiders.

No sooner had they entered the city square however, than a Gungan captain, astride a Kaadus, apprehended the party.

'Yousa in big dudu dis time Jar Jar,' the Captain said, poking Jar Jar with his power pole and herding the group to the Boss' board room. Boss Nass sat on a high bench.

The Gungan leader listened as Qui-Gon warned him of the invasion on Naboo.

"You and the Naboo form a symbiont circle. What happens to one of you will affect the other," warned Obi-Wan.

But Boss Nass was unmoved.

"Wesa no care about da Naboo," he roared, before telling the Jedi they must leave through the dangerous planet core and Jar Jar that he would be punished.

Thinking quickly, Qui-Gon told Boss Nass about the life-debt Jar Jar owed him.

Boss Nass had no choice but to let Jar Jar leave with the Jedi by submarine.

At first the journey went smoothly, although Jar Jar began to grate on Obi-Wan, particularly when he explained that he'd been banished for his clumsy ways and that he'd once crashed Boss' own craft.

But the conversation was interrupted when the sub was violently shoved by a huge Opee.

The sub creaked as the enormous fish attempted to crush it within its huge jaws, but just then a monstrous Sando monster pounced and began to eat the Opee who instantly released the sub.

"There's always a bigger fish," joked Qui-Gon as the sub zoomed down a crevasse.

On the bridge of the Federation battleship, the Viceroy was again standing before a hologram of Darth Sidious, giving him a progress report.

"Good," Sidious replied on hearing the invasion was underway. "I have the Senate bogged down in procedures.

"By the time this incident comes up for vote, they will have no choice but to accept your control of the system. Queen Amidala is young and naive," Sidious added. "Controlling her will not be difficult."

The missing Jedi – the Viceroy had been so careful not to mention them to Darth Sidious – were still deep underwater on Naboo. Their sub had suffered power failure and was leaking water.

"Stay calm. We're not in trouble yet," Qui-Gon said.

"Monsters out dare! Leakin' in here, sinkin and no power. When yousa tink wesa in trouble," Jar Jar screeched.

Ignoring the panicking Gungan, Qui-Gon worked on the sparking wires to get the sub running, as Obi-Wan flicked switches.

With a sudden roar the engines thrust to life.

Just in time, as a Colo claw fish appeared right in front of the cockpit window and would have swallowed the craft whole had it not sped away.

Meanwhile, in Theed City, Queen Amidala watched helplessly from a palace window as the troop transports carrying the invading droid army rolled into the central plaza.

Disembarking from a transport at the head of the convoy, Nute was in buoyant mood. "Aaah victory!" he breathed, seeing empty streets and the palace beyond.

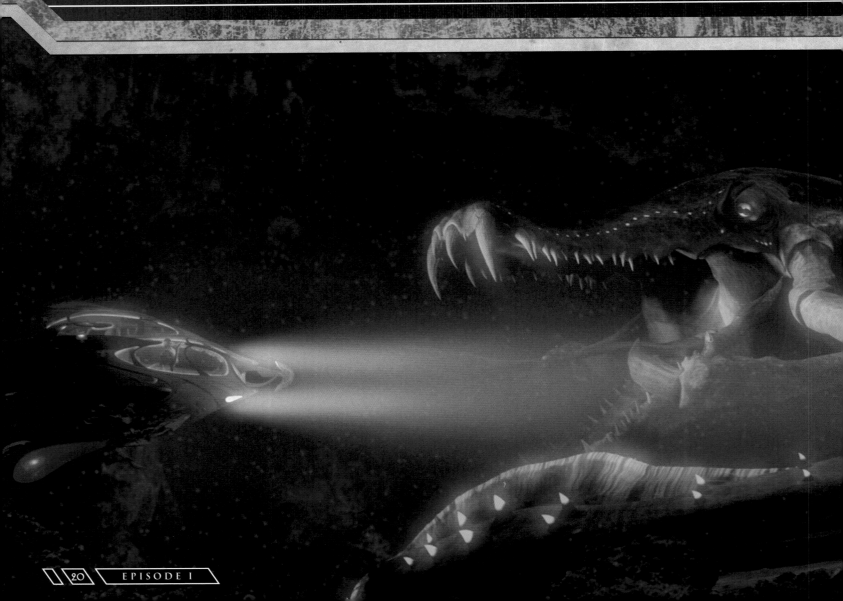

The droids took the Viceroy into the palace to see the captive Queen and her counselors.

"How will you explain this invasion to the Senate?" asked Amidala, as she was escorted down a huge stone staircase.

"The Naboo and the Federation will forge a treaty that will legitimise our occupation here. I've been assured it will be ratified by the Senate," the Viceroy told her.

"I will not co-operate," the Queen announced.

"In time the suffering of your people will persuade you to see our point of view," replied the Viceroy coldly, as the droids escorted the party outside to be processed.

At that moment, the surface of the river running through the city rippled then broke over the nose of a Gungan sub.

The Jedi and Jar Jar had made it to Theed. Within minutes the trio were on dry land.

Making their way onto a covered bridge they lay in wait for the Queen's party and as the droids escorted her under the bridge, they dropped noiselessly from above and wiped out the enemy with their lightsabers.

"We are the ambassadors for the Supreme Chancellor," Qui-Gon announced to the Queen.

"Your negotiations seem to have failed," interrupted Governor Bibble.

"They never took place," explained Qui-Gon, telling the Queen that they must make contact with the Republic.

Hearing this was impossible, Qui-Gon decided the Queen must escape with them to Coruscant.

"Then, I will plead our case before the Senate," she said bravely.

The Queen, accompanied by three of her handmaidens and her loyal Captain Panaka, followed the Jedi and Jar Jar into the main hangar that was filled with sleek chrome spacecraft.

"We need to free those pilots," Panaka said, pointing to a group of captured Naboo pilots surrounded by six battle droids.

"I'll take care of that," said Obi-Wan as he began cutting down droids. Within moments the pilots were free and the Queen and Jedi rushed on-board a spacecraft.

Pilot Ric Olie took the controls and eased the craft out of the hanger and into space. Now they needed to break through the blockade. As soon as the battleships spotted the escaping craft they began firing heavily. One explosion rocked the craft to the core. The shield generator had been hit.

"Hopefully the repair droids can fix it," Ric Olie shouted, activating the droids in the hold and ejecting them through an airlock onto the ship's wing.

"Do you have a cloaking device?" Qui-Gon asked Captain Panaka, as another deadly missile whipped past.

"No, we have no weapons. We're a non-violent people, that's why the Federation was brave enough to attack us," said Panaka.

"We're losing droids fast," cried Obi-Wan, as Federation fire blasted two astromech droids from the wing.

"If they can't get those shield generators fixed, we'll be sitting ducks," said Panaka.

Luckily one blue droid was still in place. With a twist of his tool he connected some wires and the deflector shields buzzed into place. The ship could withstand enemy fire for now, at least. But…

"There's not enough power to get us to Coruscant. The hyperdrive is leaking," said the pilot.

Qui-Gon and Obi-Wan studied a star chart and made a hasty plan. They'd land on nearby Tatooine, a small, poor, remote planet where the Trade Federation had no presence.

On a Federation battleship Viceroy Nute Gunray and Rune were again in conference with Darth Sidious' hologram.

"Destroy all high-ranking officials," Sidious ordered. "Queen Amidala, has she signed the treaty?"

"She has disappeared, my Lord," admitted Nute, nervously. "One Naboo cruiser got past the blockade."

Darth Sidious's voice cracked with rage. "Find her! I want that treaty signed."

"It's impossible to locate the ship. It's out of our range," said Nute.

"Not for a Sith" came the reply.

The hologram of a second Sith Lord appeared behind Sidious. His face was a terrifying mask of red and black lines, his eyes blazed red with yellow irises.

"This is my apprentice, Lord Maul. He will find your lost ship," said Sidious.

"This is getting out of hand, now there are two of them," Nute told Rune once the holograms had vanished.

In the Queen's quarters, Amidala had been informed of the change of plan and was readying herself, whilst at the same time making the acquaintance of the droid responsible for restoring

the ship's shields.

"It is to be commended, what is it's number?" she asked Captain Panaka.

"R2-D2, Your Highness," replied Panaka.

The Queen crouched down by the battered droid and gave her thanks.

"You have proven very loyal" she said before commanding her first handmaiden, Padmé to clean the droid up.

In the hold, Padmé oiled and scrubbed R2-D2 with the help of Jar Jar, who was doing his best to keep out of trouble.

A few hours later, the ship landed in the Tatooine desert in a swirl of dust. In the engine room, Obi-Wan was surrounded by tools.

"The hyperdrive generator is gone," he told Qui-Gon. "We'll need a new one."

"That'll complicate things," said Qui-Gon. "Don't let them send any transmissions. Be wary, I sense a disturbance in the Force."

"I feel it also Master," nodded Obi-Wan.

Qui-Gon, Jar Jar and R2-D2 made their way down the exit ramp out of the craft, but as they started onto the burning sand, a shout made them stop and turn.

Captain Panaka approached with Padmé.

"Her Highness commands you to take her handmaiden with you," he said.

When Padmé assured Qui-Gon she could take care of herself he reluctantly agreed she could accompany him to Mos Espa, Tatooine's spaceport.

The party walked through the streets until they came to a small square surrounded by junk spaceship dealers.

They headed for one of the smaller outlets. Inside they found Watto, a pudgy blue alien, flying on short little wings like a hummingbird.

"I need parts for a J-type 327 Nubian," Qui-Gon said.

"Ah yes. Nubian. We have lots of that," Watto replied, calling a disheveled looking boy from the back room and raising a hand as if to cosh him.

"What took you so long?" he grunted at the boy.

"I was cleaning the fan switches," the boy replied.

"Watch the store! I've got some selling to do," Watto commanded, heading to the yard with Qui-Gon to search for the engine part.

The boy gazed at Padmé as she wandered around the store taking in the stacks of metal components.

"Are you an angel?" he asked.

"What?" smiled Padmé, blushing under his intense gaze.

"An angel. I've heard the deep space pilots talk about them. They live on the moon of Iego, I think. "They are the most beautiful creatures in the universe. They are good and kind, and so pretty they make even the most hardened space pirate cry," the boy said.

Padmé had never met such a funny little boy.

"I'm a pilot, you know, and someday, I'm going to fly away from this place," he said proudly, explaining that he'd been on Tatooine since the age of three when Gardulla the Hutt had lost ownership of him and his mother to Watto, in a Podracing bet.

"You're a slave?" gasped Padmé.

The boy bristled. "I am a person! My name is Anakin Skywalker," he said defiantly.

Out back, Watto had found the generator Qui-Gon needed but to Qui-Gon's dismay had refused to be paid in Republic credits.

"I don't have anything else, Republic credits will be fine" Qui-Gon said, waving his hand before Watto's eyes.

Watto was having none of it.

"What do you think you are, some kinda Jedi, waving your hand around like that? I'm a Toydarian. Mind tricks don't work on me – only money," he wheezed.

"No money, no parts! No deal!" With that, Qui-Gon quickly strode in from the yard.

"We are leaving," he told Padmé and Jar Jar.

"I'm glad I met you," Anakin called to Padmé as she left.

On the busy street Qui-Gon checked in with Obi-Wan to see if there was anything of value on board they could use in exchange for the hyperdrive generator.

"Not in the amounts you're talking about," Obi-Wan admitted.

Meanwhile Jar Jar was in trouble. The greedy Gungan had spotted a dead frog on a stall and snapped out his tongue to eat it, but the vendor appeared and the frog ricocheted off into the soup of an alien lunching nearby.

"Is this yours?" roared the alien, holding up the frog and shoving Jar Jar to the ground.

Luckily Anakin was on hand.

"Careful Sebulba…" the boy said to the angry creature, who was now sitting on Jar Jar's chest. "This one's a big time outlander. I'd hate to see you diced before we race again."

"Next time we race, it will be the end of you," Sebulba grunted menacingly.

"If you weren't a slave, I'd squash you right now," he added, before slinking back to his meal.

"Your buddy here was about to be turned into orange goo," Anakin told Qui-Gon. "He picked a fight with a dangerous Dug called Sebulba."

"Thank you, my young friend," said Qui-Gon, who had arrived in time to see Anakin save Jar Jar's hide.

As the group walked through the market the wind began whipping up a dangerous sandstorm.

"Follow me," urged Anakin, rushing down a passage towards the slave quarters where he lived.

"Mom, I'm home!" cried Anakin, as he entered his hovel. The boy introduced his friends to his mother, who reluctantly welcomed them.

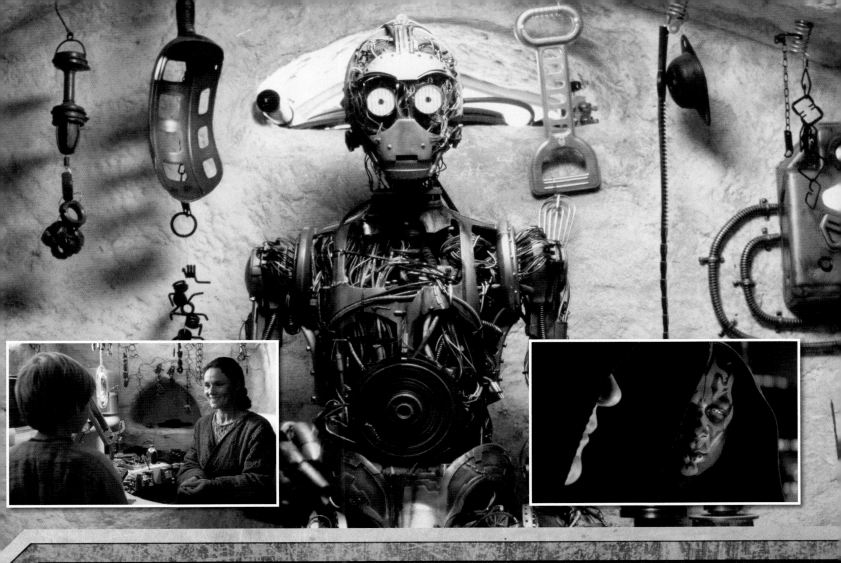

"I'm building a droid. You wanna see?" Anakin asked Padmé. He led her into his bedroom.

"Let me show you Threepio," he said, flicking the switch on a half-built protocol droid which immediately stood up and introduced itself.

"How do you do, I am C-3PO, Human Cyborg Relations. How might I serve you?" the droid asked.

"He's perfect," admitted Padmé, as she listened to Anakin's excited descriptions of the things he'd built – including a Podracer.

Meanwhile, Qui-Gon contacted Obi-Wan. Obi-Wan explained to his master that a hologram of Governor Bibble had arrived in which he pleaded with the Queen to capitulate because her people were dying in great numbers.

"The Queen is upset, but absolutely no reply was sent," Obi-Wan assured Qui-Gon.

"It sounds like bait to establish a connection trace," predicted Qui-Gon.

The wise Jedi was right.

On Coruscant, Darth Sidious and his apprentice Darth Maul were discussing their course of action.

"Tatooine is sparsely populated. If the trace was correct, I will find them quickly, Master," said Maul.

"Move against the Jedi first, then take the Queen to Naboo to sign the treaty," said Sidious.

"At last we will have revenge!"hissed Maul.

"The Republic will soon be in my control," added Sidious.

Over dinner on Tatooine, talk turned to Podracing. "Have you ever seen a Podrace?" Anakin asked Padmé, who shook her head.

"Very fast, very dangerous!" said Qui-Gon.

"I'm the only human who can do it," said Anakin.

"You must have Jedi reflexes," smiled Qui-Gon.

Anakin told Qui-Gon he knew he was a Jedi, admitting he'd caught a glimpse of Qui-Gon's lightsaber.

"I can see there's no fooling you," said Qui-Gon, explaining their predicament with the missing spaceship part.

"I can help, I can fix anything!" cried Anakin.

"I believe you can, but our first job is to acquire the parts we need," said Qui-Gon.

Anakin's mother, Shmi, explained that the junk dealer's weakness was gambling on Podracing and Anakin immediately suggested he enter his home-built Podracer in the big race the next day on Boonta Eve.

"Watto doesn't know I've built it," Anakin told Qui-Gon. "You could make him think it was yours and you could get him to let me pilot it for you. The prize money would more than pay for the parts."

Shmi looked so appalled at the thought that Padmé and Qui-Gon said they'd find another way. Then Shmi capitulated.

"Ani's right. There is no other way. I may not like it, but he can help you. He was meant to help you."

The plan was on.

Next day at the store, Watto took some convincing to take the wager but greed got the better of him.

"So, you supply the Podracer and entry fee; I supply the boy. We split the winnings fifty-fifty," he laughed.

"I suggest you front the cash for entry. If we win, you keep all the winnings, minus the cost of the parts I need. If we lose, you keep my ship. Either way, you win," coaxed Qui-Gon.

"Deal," agreed Watto, taking the bait. While Padmé, Anakin, Jar Jar and R2-D2 worked on the engines of the Podracer in the courtyard, Qui-Gon spoke to Shmi.

"You should be proud of your son," he told her. "He gives without thought of reward."

"He knows nothing of greed," said Shmi. "He has..."

"Special powers," finished Qui-Gon. "He can see things before they happen. That's why he appears to have such quick reflexes. It is a Jedi trait."

"He deserves better than a slave's life" murmured Shmi.

"The Force is unusually strong with him, that much is clear," said Qui-Gon.

Shmi told Qui-Gon about the mysterious father-less circumstances surrounding Anakin's birth.

"Can you help him?" she asked.

"I'm afraid not," said Qui-Gon. "In the Republic, we would have identified him early but it's too late for him now, he's too old."

A noise from outside caught Qui-Gon's attention and he walked into the courtyard to check out the commotion.

Jar Jar had caught his tongue in the Podracer's energy plate and hand in the afterburner.

"You don't even know if this thing will run," mocked Kitster, one of Anakin's friends, who had turned up to watch him work.

"I think it's time we found out," said Qui-Gon.

"Use this power charge."

Anakin slapped the power pack into the dashboard and the engines ignited with a roar.

That night, after tending to one of Anakin's cuts, Qui-Gon sent a sample of his blood over to Obi-Wan asking for a midi-chlorian count. The results were incredible.

"The reading's off the chart. Over twenty thousand… even Master Yoda doesn't have a midi-chlorian count that high," exclaimed Obi-Wan.

"No Jedi has," mused Qui-Gon, staring into the distance.

As Qui-Gon pondered Anakin's future, a lone Sith spacecraft landed noiselessly in the desert.

A cloaked figure emerged and walked to the edge of a dune. Seeing the lights of three cities in the distance, Darth Maul summoned three probe droids from the craft. They flew off to find the Jedi.

Next day, Qui-Gon left the slave quarters early and headed for the arena. There he met Watto.

"I want to see your spaceship the moment the race is over," Watto said.

Qui-Gon urged patience. "You'll have your winnings before the suns set, and we'll be far away from here."

"Not if your ship belongs to me," Watto chuckled. "Don't get me wrong. I have great faith in the boy. He's a credit to your race, but I'm betting heavily on Sebulba."

Sensing a way to free Anakin and Shmi, Qui-Gon moved fast.

"I'll take that bet," he told Watto. "I'll wager my new Podracer against the boy and his mother."

"No Podracer's worth two slaves. One slave or nothing," said Watto, pulling a small chance cube from his pocket.

"Blue it's the boy, red his mother…" Watto tossed the cube. Qui-Gon lifted his palm and the cube stopped blue side-up.

Watto was furious. "You won this small toss, outlander, but you won't win the race." He flapped angrily out of the hangar passing Anakin, Padmé, Shmi and Kitster on the way out.

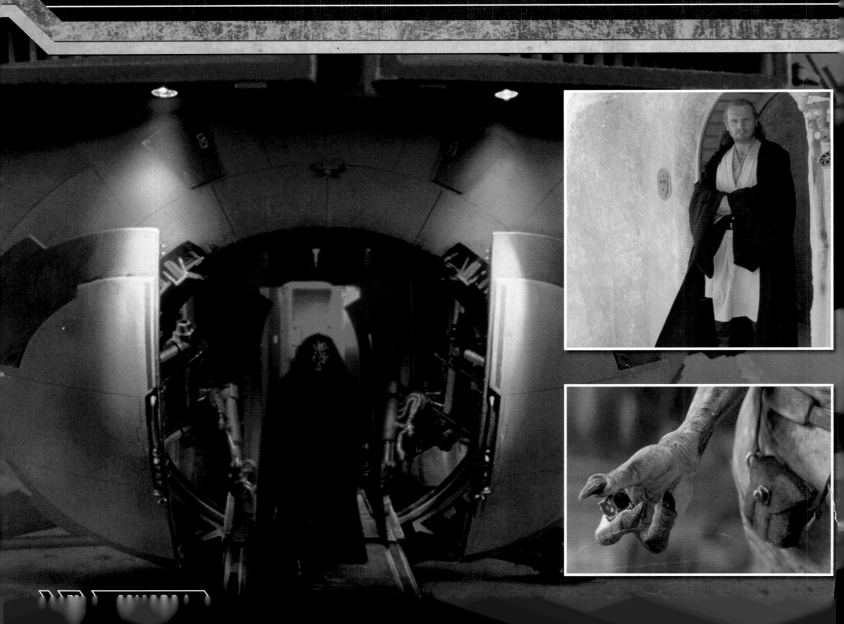

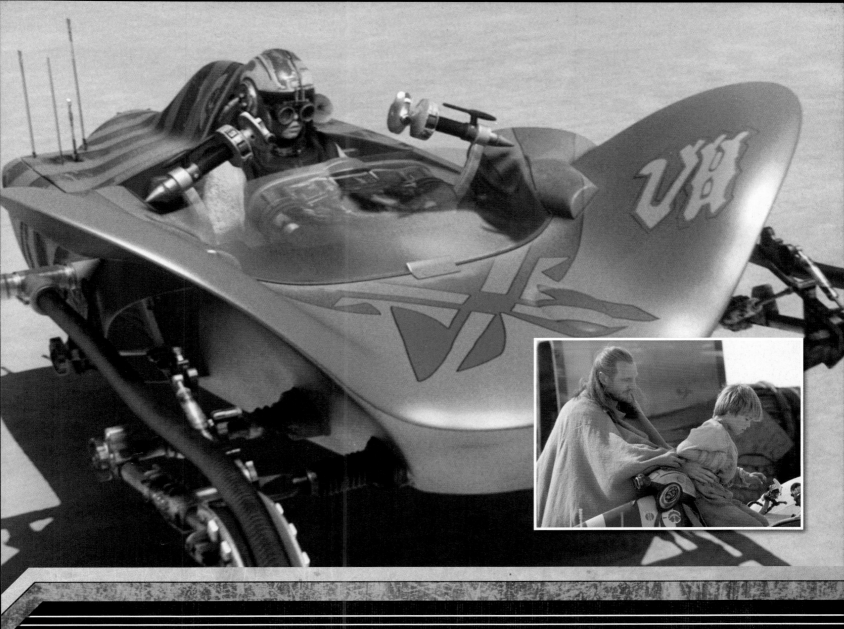

"Better stop your friend's betting, or I'll end up owning him, too," Watto told a confused Anakin.

"I'm sure you'll do it this time Ani," Kitster told his friend.

"Do what?" Padmé asked.

"Finish the race," Kitster replied.

Padmé was shocked. "You've never won a race?" she asked.

Anakin had to admit that not only had he never won – he'd never even finished!

"But I will this time," he said.

"Of course you will," nodded Qui-Gon.

As Anakin and the other pilots carried out last minute checks on their Podracers, the announcers talked to the thousands of spectators gathered in the amphitheatre through the competitors.

"I see Ben Quadinaros from the Tund system and Gasgano in his new Ord Pedrovia, Two-time winner, Bos Roar, the reigning champion Sebulba and a late entry, Anakin Skywalker, a local boy."

The crowd went wild. All the pilots bowed low as Jabba The Hutt entered the royal box to start the race.

Down on the start line Qui-Gon, Jar Jar, Shmi and Padmé wished Anakin luck.

"May the Force be with you," uttered Qui-Gon.

"You carry all our hopes," whispered Padmé, kissing Anakin on the cheek.

"I won't let you down," said Anakin.

But he hadn't noticed Sebulba ripping a protruding part from the engine of his Podracer.

"You won't walk away from this one, slave scum," Sebulba hissed.

"Kaa bazza kundee hodrudda," announced Jabba. "Let the challenge begin."

With an earth-pounding roar the engines revved and the Podracers zoomed off – all except one. Anakin's engine flooded then stalled – but finally he too sped into the distance.

The race was fast and furious. Sebulba drove his Podracer into Mawhonic forcing him to crash into a large rock formation, while Gasgano blocked Anakin.

But with some tricky manoeuvres Anakin eventually sailed over the top of Gasgano and sped away. Next, all the racers had to contend with Tusken Raiders taking pot shots at them from a vantage point on canyon dune turn. Anakin swerved left and right to avoid the blasts, but other racers were not so lucky.

As Anakin gained ground on the second lap, Sebulba destroyed contender after contender with a mixture of skill and devious cunning.

He cut Obitoki's engine off using his side exhaust and when Terter got too close for comfort Sebulba dispatched him by breaking a part off his own Podracer and throwing it into Terter's engine.

Terter veered into Anakin and unhooked one of the main straps linking Anakin's Podracer to his engines.

For several unbearable moments Anakin seemed lost. His Podracer whipped about wildly, the broken engine strap flailing. Then he made one final grab for the strap and managed to reattach it.

On the third and final lap Anakin was directly behind Sebulba but the devious alien had one last trick up his sleeve.

As they headed side by side up the final stretch, Sebulba crashed repeatedly into Anakin. The steering rods of both Podracers hooked together.

Anakin tried valiantly to pull away, suddenly his steering arm broke sending his Podracer spinning over and over.

Sebulba grinned, sure of victory, but the sudden tension release sent his pod catapulting into an ancient statue.

Both engines exploded and he skidded to a humiliating stop. With one final monumental effort, Anakin regained control of his Podracer and raced proudly over the finish line.

"Whenever you gamble, my friend, eventually, you'll lose," Qui-Gon told a seething Watto. "Bring the parts to the main hanger. I'll come by your shop later so you can release the boy."

Qui-Gon strode away to congratulate Anakin with Watto's whining voice in his ears, but he hadn't noticed Darth Maul's probe droid monitoring him from a distance.

In the hangar, Jar Jar swung Anakin high in the air while Padmé and Shmi hugged him.

"We owe you everything," smiled Padmé.

"Just feeling this good was worth it," grinned Anakin.

When Qui-Gon had returned the hyperdrive generator to the ship and asked Obi-Wan to install it, he headed back to the slave quarters to find Anakin.

"These are yours. We sold the Podracer," Qui-Gon told Anakin and Shmi, tipping a handful of coins onto the table.

"And no longer a slave," he added.

"Now you can make your dreams come true Ani," said Shmi.

She turned to Qui-Gon. "Is he to become a Jedi?" Qui-Gon nodded.

"Our meeting was not a coincidence. Nothing happens by accident. You are strong with the Force, but you may not be accepted by the Council," he warned.

Anakin was beside himself. "Mighty blasters! It's what I've always dreamed about," he beamed. Then his face darkened when he realised his mother would have to remain with Watto.

"It is time for you to let go of me," said Shmi. "Listen to your feelings, Ani, you know what's right."

Anakin gave his mother a last hug. "I will become a Jedi and I will come back and free you. I promise," he told her.

"No matter where you are, my love will be with you," she told him. "Now be brave and don't look back."

As Anakin and Qui-Gon made their way out of the city, something caught Qui-Gon's eye.

Suddenly, without breaking his stride, he ignited his lightsaber, swung round and cut a lurking probe droid in half.

"What is it?" Anakin asked.

"Probe droid. Very unusual. Come on," said Qui Gon, catching Anakin's arm and breaking into a run.

The pair made it back to the desert and were nearing the spacecraft when a cloaked figure appeared in the distance on a speeder bike. It was Darth Maul.

"Drop," Qui-Gon ordered and Anakin dropped to the ground just as Darth Maul swept over him.

"Get to the ship! Take off," Qui Gon yelled as he and Darth Maul locked lightsabers. Anakin ran into the spaceship and onto the bridge.

"Qui-Gon is in trouble, he says to take off," Anakin told the pilot who, on Obi-Wan's orders, flew towards the dust cloud rising where Qui-Gon and Darth Maul were locked in combat.

As the ship flew over their heads Qui-Gon leapt in the air and landed on the spacecraft's ramp. The ship sped into hyperspace. They'd escaped the Sith – for now!

While most of the crew slept on the ship, Padmé checked the Naboo Governor's plea recording.

Suddenly she noticed Anakin shivering and gave him her jacket.

"You seem sad," Anakin said.

"The Queen is worried," Padmé replied. "Her people are suffering, dying. She must convince the Senate to intervene, or I'm not sure what will happen."

To cheer Padmé up, Anakin gave her a pendant he'd carved from a snippet of japor wood.

"It's beautiful, but I don't need this to remember you," she said.

"Many things will change when we reach the capital. But my caring for you will always remain."

Seeing tears in Anakin's eyes, Padmé enveloped him in a hug. For all his bravery, Anakin missed his mother.

A few hours later the Naboo spacecraft finally reached Coruscant. When they'd docked on a platform and disembarked, they were met by Senator Palpatine and Chancellor Valorum.

Valorum immediately offered his support over the invasion and explained he'd called an urgent meeting of the Senate. But Palpatine waited until he had Amidala alone to lay his cards on the table.

"I must be frank, Your Majesty, there is little chance the Senate will act on the invasion," he said. "The Chancellor has little real power and is mired by accusations of corruption." He then suggested they push for the election of a stronger Supreme Chancellor. "Call for a vote of no confidence in Chancellor Valorum," he urged.

Next morning Qui-Gon stood before the Jedi Council to update them on the attack by Darth Maul.

"My only conclusion can be that it was a Sith Lord," he told the twelve Jedi seated in a semi-circle before him.

"Impossible! The Sith have been extinct for a millennium," said one member.

"The very Republic is threatened if involved the Sith are," said Master Yoda. "Hard to see, the dark side is. Discover who this assassin is, we must," he added.

The council agreed Qui-Gon was to stay with Amidala to protect her.

Qui-Gon then tackled his second, trickier subject: Anakin.

"With your permission, my Master," he asked Yoda. "I have encountered a vergence in the force. A boy. His cells have the highest concentration of midi-chlorians I have seen in a life form. It is possible he was conceived by the midi-chlorians."

"You're referring to the prophesy of the one who will bring balance to the Force. You believe it's this boy?" asked senior Jedi, Mace Windu.

"I request the boy be tested," said Qui-Gon.

Yoda, delivered his verdict. "Tested, he will be."

Meanwhile, Amidala was putting her case to the Senate, but to her astonishment, Chancellor Valorum listened to denials from members of the Trade Federation and requested that she allow a commission to bring the Senate proof the invasion had happened.

"I have come before you to resolve this attack on our sovereignty now," she cried angrily. "I was not elected to watch my people die while you discuss this invasion in a committee.

"If this body is not capable of action, I suggest new leadership is needed. I move for a 'Vote of No Confidence' in Chancellor Valorum's leadership."

Palpatine turned to the Queen, dripping his self-serving advice in her ears.

"The tide is with us… they will elect a new, strong Chancellor, one who will not let our tragedy continue."

The chamber rang out with chants of "Vote Now, Vote Now," as Valorum sank defeated into his chair.

Next day Anakin was called to the Jedi Temple. Mace Windu viewed a succession of images on a small screen in his hand while Anakin attempted to use his powers to define them.

"A ship… a cup… a speeder…" he told Mace.

"Good, young one. How feel you?" asked Yoda.

"Cold, sir," replied Anakin.

"Afraid are you?" asked Yoda

"No, sir," Anakin countered.

But Yoda and the Council were not convinced.

"Afraid to lose your mother, I think," Yoda said.

This made Anakin angry.

"What's that got to do with anything?" he asked.

"Everything," said Yoda. "Fear is the path to the dark side. Fear leads to anger, anger leads to hate, hate leads to suffering. I sense much fear in you."

Later Captain Panaka rushed into the Queen's quarters with news.

"Your Highness, Senator Palpatine has been nominated to succeed Chancellor Valorum."

"A surprise to be sure, but a welcome one," said Palpatine.

But Amidala was not calmed by the news.

"With the Senate in transition, there is nothing more I can do here. Senator, this is your arena. I feel I must return to mine. I have decided to go back to Naboo. My place is with my people."

Ignoring Palpatine's pleas that a return would put her in danger, the brave Queen ordered Panaka to have her ship ready.

"It is clear to me now that the Republic no longer functions. I pray you will bring sanity and compassion back to the Senate," she told Palpatine.

By evening, the Jedi Council had come to its decision. Yoda summoned Anakin, Obi-Wan and Qui-Gon to the Temple.

"The Force is strong with him," said Mace Windu.

"He is to be trained then?" asked Qui-Gon.

"No," came the answer. Tears of disappointment pricked in Anakin's eyes while Qui-Gon stepped forward, aghast at the decision.

"He is too old. There is already too much anger in him," explained Mace.

"He is the Chosen One. You must see it," said Qui-Gon. Then Yoda spoke up.

"Clouded, this boy's future is."

Qui-Gon put his hands on Anakin's shoulders.

"I will train him, then."

Obi-Wan stared at Qui-Gon in surprise.

"An apprentice, you have, Qui-Gon. Impossible, to take on a second," said Yoda.

But Qui-Gon had an answer. "Obi-Wan is ready. There is little more he can learn from me."

Yoda decided that Anakin's fate would be decided later. He ordered Qui-Gon and Obi-Wan to accompany the Queen back to Naboo, to discover the identity of the dark Sith warrior.

As Obi-Wan and Qui-Gon crossed the landing platform towards the Naboo spacecraft where the Queen waited, they discussed Anakin.

"The boy is dangerous," Obi-Wan warned.

"They all sense it. Why can't you?"

"His fate is uncertain, not dangerous. The Council wi decide Anakin's future, that should be enough for you Now get on board," ordered Qui-Gon sternly.

Obi-Wan obeyed reluctantly and R2-D2 followed him into the ship.

Then Anakin piped up. "What are midi-chlorians? he asked.

"A microscopic life form that resides in all living cells and communicates with the Force. Without the midi-chlorians life could not exist, and we would hav no knowledge of the Force," explained Qui-Gon. "Whe you learn to quiet your mind, you will hear them."

"Wesa goen home," screeched Jar Jar as the the ship blasted into space.

In the Queen's throne room on Naboo, Nute Gunray was in audience with Darth Sidious' hologram.

"Viceroy, is the planet secure?" Sidious asked.

"Yes, my Lord," Nute answered.

"Good. I will see to it that in the Senate things stay as they are. I am sending Darth Maul to join you and deal with the Jedi," said Sidious

In Amidala's chambers on board the spacecraft, her staff and the Jedi tried to reason with her.

"The moment we land, the Federation will arrest you and force you to sign the treaty," warned Captain Panaka.

"I agree. I'm not sure what you hope to accomplish by this. I cannot fight a war for you, only protect you," added Qui-Gon.

But Amidala had a plan. She called for Jar Jar.

"Mesa, Your Highness?" asked the surprised Gungan.

"I need your help," said the Queen.

When the spacecraft landed on the edge of the swamp, Jar Jar made his way to the Gungan City.

While they awaited his return, Obi-Wan begged Qui-Gon's forgiveness.

"I'm sorry for my behaviour, Master. It's not my place to disagree with you about the boy. I am grateful you think I'm ready for the trials," said Obi-Wan.

"You've been a good apprentice" Qui-Gon told Obi-Wan. "You are wiser than I am. You will become a great Jedi Knight."

At that moment Jar Jar emerged from the lake. "Dare-sa nobody dare," he said. "Gungan hidden. When in trouble, got to sacred place." Then he strode off into the forest to seek out his people.

The Queen and her staff, Anakin, Qui-Gon, Obi-Wan and R2-D2 followed Jar Jar through thick undergrowth, but at last they came to a clearing full of Gungan refugees.

At one end, Boss Nass stood amid the ruins of a grand temple.

"Who's da uss-en others?" spat the Gungan leader.

Queen Amidala stepped forward and introduced herself. "I come before you in peace," she said.

Boss Nass was angry, blaming the Naboo for bringing the invasion upon the Gungans. "Yousa bringen da mackineeks. Day busten uss-en. Yousa all die'n, mesa tink," he roared.

Padmé stepped forward. "Your Honour…" she ventured.

"Whosa dis?" Boss Nass was confused.

Then Padmé dropped a bombshell.

"I am Queen Amidala." She pointed to her handmaiden, Sabe, dressed as the Queen. "This is my decoy, my protection, my loyal bodyguard," she explained.

While Anakin looked stunned, the Jedi exchanged knowing glances.

Padmé – the real Queen Amidala – then delivered a humble speech explaining the situation.

"Our two great societies have always lived in peace. The Trade Federation has destroyed all that we have worked so hard to build. If we do not act quickly, all will be lost. I beg you to help us," she pleaded.

She dropped to her knees followed by her entourage and the Jedi.

There was a pause then Boss Nass opened his fleshy mouth and let out a howl of laughter.

"Yousa no tinken yousa greater den da Gungans. Mesa like dis! Maybe wesa bein friends."

The alliance was formed and a grateful Boss Nass made Jar Jar a general.

Hiding out at the edge of the forest, Padmé, Captain Panaka and the Jedi discussed tactics.

"The Federation army's much larger than we thought. Your Highness, this is a battle I do not think we can win," said the worried captain.

"The battle is a diversion," snapped the Queen. "The Gungans must draw the droid army away from the cities.

"We can enter the city using the secret passages on the waterfall side. Once we get to the main palace entrance, Captain Panaka will create a diversion so we can capture the Viceroy."

"Wesa ready to do are-sa part," nodded Boss Nass. Padmé then explained the rest of the plan. They would send some Naboo pilots to knock out the droid control ship orbiting the planet, thus disabling the droids.

"If the Viceroy escapes, Your Highness, he will return with another droid army," warned Obi-Wan.

"That is why we must not fail to get the Viceroy," said Padmé.

In the throne room, Nute Gunray received his Sith visitor. Darth Maul walked beside him as Darth Sidious addressed them via hologram.

"We are sending all troops to meet this army of hers assembling near the swamp. We do not expect much resistance," said Nute.

"I feel there is more to this, my Master. The Jedi may be using the Queen for their own purposes," said Maul.

Darth Sidious shook his head.

"The Jedi cannot become involved. They can only protect the Queen. Even Qui-Gon Jinn will not break that covenant."

"I have your approval to proceed?" asked Nute.

"Wipe them out. All of them." Sidious's tone was ice cold.

On the vast plains outside the city of Theed, the Gungan army waited. Mounted soldiers rode huge lizard-like Fambaas, while marching warriors held shield generators.

Enormous bubble-like shields covered the troops like a protective umbrella.

Through the hazy screen, the waiting Gungan could just make out a line of Federation tanks stretching across the ridge on the horizon. The droids began firing missiles at the Gungans but the bubble shield held fast and nothing could penetrate.

When the droid commander realised this he gave the cease-fire order. Instead, huge numbers of troop transports began rolling out row after row of droids.

Inside the shield, nervous Gungans gulped and eyed each other with fear.

"Steady," called Jar Jar, holding his nerve and scanning the ever-increasing number of droids marching towards them.

Inside the city things were equally tense. Padmé, Anakin, R2 and the Jedi stealthily made their way into the main hangar.

Twenty Naboo guards and pilots followed them.

"Once we get inside Ani, you find a safe place to hide," Qui-Gon told Anakin.

Then Padmé gave the signal to Captain Panaka, who began his diversion on the other side of the square, firing on the droids in the plaza to distract them.

Padmé's group ran into the hangar and immediately began firing on the battle droids manning the grounded Naboo spacecraft.

Naboo pilots climbed into their craft and began taking off.

The gunfire was so heavy Anakin could find no safe place to hide except a lone craft left by the pilots.

He climbed in, followed by R2-D2 and began pressing buttons to close the cockpit.

The hangar was now deserted except for the Jedi and the Sith and the air was filled with the sound of clashing lightsabers.

Darth Maul's horned skull bobbed and weaved as he ducked blows from Obi-Wan and Qui-Gon.

With awesome skill the Sith wielded his double-ended lightsaber, parrying and striking at the same time.

Maul jumped onto the narrow bridge of the Theed power generator. The Jedi followed and the fight continued, one Jedi in front and one behind the fearsome Sith.

On the battlefield the Gungans did their best to repel the droid attack, firing energy balls into their ranks.

Jar Jar's clumsiness actually worked for him in battle. First he got caught in the wiring of a wrecked droid, blasting several droids accidentally as he dragged the torso around.

Then he hitched a ride on a wagon accidentally releasing the entire load of energy balls, which pole-axed several deadly destroyer droids.

In space, Anakin's autopilot took him towards the droid control battleship. Within moments he was in the middle of the battle.

R2 succeeded in giving Anakin manual control just in time.

An enemy fighter came into his sights. He tried to fire but accidentally accelerated past the ship that made him the target. R2 beeped at Anakin.

"Go back?" Anakin yelled. "Qui-Gon told me to stay in this cockpit and that's just what I'm going to do."

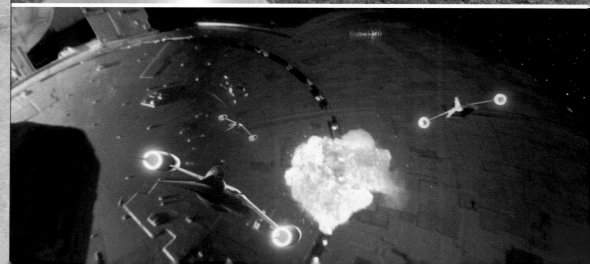

He tried rolling the craft but instead sped dangerously out of control and into the battleship's hangar.

"This is not good," he cried, as the craft screeched to a halt and droids surrounded them.

On Naboo, Darth Maul landed a devastating blow on Obi-Wan that sent the young Jedi flying over the edge of the bridge and into the void.

Luckily he managed to catch the edge of a ledge below and cling on, as Qui-Gon and Darth Maul disappeared through a doorway into another chamber.

Obi-Wan scrabbled up just in time to see Qui-Gon caught between two electron ray gates. The Jedi dropped to his knee and closed his eyes, tapping into the Force to predict Maul's next move.

Suddenly the ray gates lifted and Qui-Gon ran through and into combat with Darth Maul.

This still left Obi-Wan on the other side of the first gate, unable to help his Master, as Qui-Gon deflected blow after blow from Maul's weapon.

As Obi-Wan gazed on helplessly, Maul whipped around and with one lethal thrust ran his lightsabre through Qui-Gon's chest.

The Jedi slumped to the floor in a heap.

"No!" screamed Obi-Wan.

In the palace, Padmé and her guards fought valiantly, but were captured by destroyer droids just outside the throne room.

On the plains the Gungans had been overrun. Things looked bad for the allies. Very bad.

Ten battle droids brought Padmé before the Viceroy and Rune.

"Your little insurrection is at an end, Your Highness," smirked Nute. "Time for you to sign the treaty and end this pointless debate in the Senate."

At that moment Sabe, the handmaiden decoy dressed as the Queen, appeared in the doorway with several troops.

"I will not be signing any treaty, Viceroy, because you have lost," Sabe called in her most regal voice.

The Viceroy looked up in confusion to see a second Queen, but quickly gathered his thoughts.

"After her," he ordered his droids, pointing at Sabe. "This one is just a decoy!"

The droids rushed out of the room, chasing the fake Queen.

"Your Queen will not get away with this," Nute told Padmé, who pretended to be defeated and slumped down on her throne.

As she did, she hit a security button that opened a secret compartment in her desk. She withdrew two pistols, arming herself and throwing one to Captain Panaka.

Together they blasted the remaining droids, sealed themselves and the Viceroy in the room and ordered their guards to encircle the stunned Viceroy and his assistant.

"Now, Viceroy, we will discuss a new treaty," said Padmé.

"Don't be absurd. It won't be long before hundreds of destroyer droids break in here to rescue us," mocked Nute.

In the hangar, Obi-Wan finally met Darth Maul one-on-one. The Sith Lord used all his power to attack the young Jedi who stubbornly refused to be beaten.

Both the Jedi and the Sith circled each other endlessly, using the Force to fling objects at each other as they fought.

Suddenly Darth Maul caught Obi-Wan off-guard, landing a blow that sent the Jedi over the edge of the walkway into the pit below. He grabbed a nozzle on the side of the pit.

With an evil grin, Darth Maul looked down at Obi-Wan and then kicked Obi-Wan's lightsaber down

the shaft. All seemed lost, but as the Sith Lord went in for the kill Obi-Wan summoned all his powers and launched himself out of the pit. He called Qui-Gon's lightsaber to him and grabbed Darth Maul.

The young Jedi thrust his lightsaber into the air and swung it with a vengeance, cutting down the Sith in one stroke.

With a blood-curdling cry, Darth Maul toppled over the edge into the pit, to meet his death.

Obi-Wan rushed over to Qui-Gon who lay dying on the platform.

"Master! Master!" he said, cradling Qui-Gon's head.

"It is too late," Qui-Gon whispered.

Obi-Wan refused to believe this was the end for the one who had trained and nurtured him for so long.

"No!" he cried.

But Qui-Gon was fading.

"Obi-Wan, promise," Qui-Gon said.

"Promise me you'll train the boy…"

"Yes Master," agreed Obi-Wan.

"He is the Chosen One. He will bring balance… train him," said Qui-Gon as his eyes closed, his head fell to one side and his last breath rattled from his body.

Obi-Wan hugged his Master tightly for what seemed like an age, quietly weeping.

In the Federation hangar, Anakin peeped over the edge of his cockpit at the battle droids surrounding his ship.

"This is not good," he hissed to R2, who beeped in reply.

Anakin checked the dashboard where several red lights flashed ominously.

"The systems are still overheated," he told R2.

At that point the captain of the battle droids approached the ship and spied R2.

"Where's your pilot?" he asked.

R2 just whistled.

"Let me see your identification," ordered the droid aiming his weapon straight at R2.

In that instant Anakin saw the dashboard lights go from red to green.

"We have ignition," he said, flipping the switch that started the engines.

"Come out of there or we'll blast you," the droid ordered Anakin.

"Not if I can help it! Shields up," the boy replied.

He flipped another switch and the ship levitated, knocking the droid captain over.

Other droids fired but their lasers were deflected by the ship's shields.

"This should stop them," said Anakin, rotating the ship and firing at the same time.

He began moving around the edge of the hangar popping off torpedos.

From their position outside the battleship the Naboo pilots watched in astonishment.

"What's that? It's blowing up from the inside," said one.

"Look! One of ours, out of the main hold," said another, as Anakin's ship flew out moments before the battleship exploded in a huge fireball.

The pilots cheered while down on the ground the droids, starved of power from the control ship, hissed, fizzed and fell over.

The next day the Supreme Chancellor's grand cruiser landed in the courtyard of the main hangar.

"Now, Viceroy, you are going to have to go back to the Senate and explain all this," said Padmé Amidala.

"I think you can kiss your trade franchise goodbye," added Captain Panaka.

The Viceroy and Rune looked downcast and headed toward the cruiser.

Obi-Wan and Captain Panaka steered the Neimoidians toward the ship as Grand Chancellor Palpatine and his guards descended, followed by Yoda and several Jedi Masters.

"We are indebted to you for yourbravery Obi-Wan Kenobi," Palpatine said as Obi-Wan bowed low.

"And you young Skywalker, we shall watch your career with great interest," Palpatine continued, placing a hand on Anakin's shoulder

"Congratulations on your election, Chancellor," said Amidala.

"Your boldness has saved our people, Your Majesty. It is you who should be congratulated," smiled Palpatine. "Together we shall bring peace and prosperity to the Republic."

Later that day in the turret room of Naboo Palace, Obi-Wan Kenobi knelt before Yoda.

"Confer on you, the level of Jedi Knight, the Council does. But agree with your taking this boy as your Padawan learner, I do not," croaked the Jedi Master.

"Qui-Gon believed in him," answered Obi-Wan.

"The Chosen One the boy may be. Nevertheless, grave danger I fear in his training," said Yoda.

"I gave Qui-Gon my word," cried Obi-Wan. "I will train Anakin. Without the approval of the Council if I must."

Yoda grunted in frustration. "Qui-Gon's defiance I sense in you. Need that, you do not."

There was a long pause, then Yoda turned back to Obi-Wan.

"Agree, the Council does. Your apprentice, young Skywalker will be."

Obi-Wan bowed his head in gratitude.

That night in the central plaza, Qui-Gon was given a hero's funeral.

The Jedi Council, Queen, Senator Palpatine, Naboo and Gungan troops watched sombrely, as flames leapt up from the funeral pyre. Jar Jar let out a whimper.

"He is one with the Force, Anakin. You must let go," Obi-Wan told Anakin who looked devastated by the loss of his mentor.

"What will happen to me now?" the boy asked.

"Council have granted me permission to train you. You will become a Jedi, I promise," soothed Obi-Wan.

Mace Windu turned his face from the pyre to face Yoda.

"There is no doubt. The mysterious warrior was a Sith," he said.

"Always two there are… no more, no less. A master and an apprentice," Yoda replied.

Mace Windu nodded, his face was grave.

"But which one was destroyed, the master or the apprentice?"

The sun rose and with it dawned a new age on Naboo.

The central plaza had been decked with colourful flags and the people, freed from oppression, lined the streets as a triumphant procession made it's way to the Royal Palace.

Horns sounded, children threw confetti and the cheers grew louder still as the Gungans approached, headed by Boss Nass and Jar Jar Binks, both mounted on Kaadu.

Reaching the palace Boss Nass jumped effortlessly from his Kaadu, while true to form, Jar Jar got his foot caught in a stirrup and hopped clumsily around.

The Gungan leader and Generals made their way up the stone steps to the palace where Queen Amidala waited, looking beautiful in a flowing white gown.

On one side of her stood her loyal captain, handmaidens and guards, and on the other Obi-Wan, Anakin and Senator Palpatine.

Boss Nass and Amidala greeted each other warmly and Amidala handed Nass a crystal Globe to mark their friendship.

"Peace," roared Boss Nass, holding it aloft.

As the crowd cheers reached a deafening crescendo, Amidala turned to Anakin and smiled.

Thanks to Anakin and the Jedi, peace had indeed returned to Naboo.

PADMÉ AMIDALA

Padmé was identified as one of the best and brightest of Naboo when she was just a child. Due to her prodigious talent and in-depth training, she became the supervisor of the planet's capital city of Theed when she was only 12 years old. At the same time she adopted a 'name of state': Amidala. Just two years later the population recognised that she was far wiser than her years would suggest and elected her the Queen of Naboo. In keeping with tradition, she embraced ornate costumes and extreme makeup that disguised her true appearance while giving her an aura of both splendour and beauty.

Not long after Padmé takes the throne, the Trade Federation blockades Naboo to protest the taxation of trade routes. The young Queen is an idealist and a great believer in the power of democracy. Because of this she is certain the Galactic Senate and the Jedi will quickly and inevitably come to the aid of her planet. She is dismayed to discover that politics and bureaucracy get in the way. This leads her to help Naboo native Senator Palpatine become Supreme Chancellor of the Senate, when she proposes a Vote of No Confidence in his predecessor, Chancellor Valorum.

After her time as Queen, she becomes a Senator herself, doing her best to bring sanity and order to the galaxy. With corruption growing and the Sith secretly sowing the seeds of discord, she is increasingly infuriated by the erosion of democracy. Padmé finds it difficult to accept the way her fellow Senators are willing to give up freedoms for the illusion of security. In spite of the increasingly grave Separatist problem, she continues to believe that diplomacy and negotiation are the way forward.

After reconnecting with Jedi Anakin Skywalker – whom Padmé first met when he was just a young boy on Tatooine – she is surprised to find herself falling deeply in love with him. The relationship is a forbidden one as it goes against Jedi Code. Padmé cannot deny her feelings though and the pair marry in secret.

DID YOU KNOW?

Playing Padmé Amidala's decoy and handmaiden, Sabé, was one of the first roles for Keira Knightley, before she went on to international superstardom.

DARTH MAUL

The Sith have been part of Jedi legend for thousands of years, but none have been seen for a millennia until Qui-Gon Jinn and Obi-Wan Kenobi encounter Darth Maul on Tatooine. Originally from the planet of Dathomir, Maul was taken in by Darth Sidious as an infant and secretly trained in all aspects of the dark side of the Force. Extremely dedicated to the Sith, Maul proved himself by undergoing an agonising Sith tattooing process, which helped give him his truly fearsome visage (the tattoos actually cover his entire body).

An acrobatic and formidable fighter who uses a double-bladed lightsaber, he is an impressive warrior whether he uses one blade or two. Fuelled by rage and an absolute obedience to Darth Sidious, Maul is keen to destroy the Jedi Order and restore power to the Sith. However even Darth Maul's Master recognises that his apprentice's biggest flaw is his hubris.

After taking on several covert missions for Sidious, Maul's existence is revealed to the Jedi when he is dispatched to kill Qui-Gon Jinn and Obi-Wan Kenobi, as well as to recapture Queen Amidala after she slips through the Trade Federation's blockade of her planet. He fails in his quest, allowing Qui-Gon to report the resurgence of the Sith to the Jedi Council.

Keen to remedy his previous failure, Maul faces Qui-Gon and Obi-Wan again on Naboo. Through a careful balance of defensive tactics and savage attacks, Maul gains the upper hand and strikes down Qui-Gon. It is an impressive feat, as Qui-Gon is renowned as one of the best lightsaber fighters in the Jedi order. Obi-Wan proves a tougher challenge, as the Jedi uses not only his battle training but also his knowledge of the Force to take Darth Maul by surprise and slice him in two.

DID YOU KNOW?

Darth Maul's eyes are far more sensitive to light than a human's.

SHMI SKYWALKER

Anakin's mother was born free, but her family was kidnapped by pirates when she was young. She was separated from her parents and sold into slavery. Shmi has had various owners, some of whom treated her better than others. She nearly gained her freedom when she was owned by Pi-Lippa, as he taught her various technical skills and promised to eventually free her. Sadly, he died before he could fulfil his promise.

During her time as the property of Gardulla the Hutt, she mysteriously became pregnant, though there had been no one to father the child. Having a son gives Shmi's life extra meaning and she works incredibly hard to provide Anakin with a good life. This is made both easier and more difficult after the junk dealer Watto wins Shmi and Anakin from Gardulla in a bet. Watto is cruel and rough, but he does allow her a small amount of independence (tempered by a device that will kill her if she tries to escape). He even permits her to earn a small amount of money cleaning computer memory devices when she isn't working for her master.

Shmi understands that her son has special gifts, although she desperately wishes that his almost preternatural skills didn't make him so good at Podracing, as she is terrified every time Watto makes him compete. She isn't surprised when Qui-Gon informs her that Anakin is sensitive to the Force, and is pleased that the Jedi can provide her son with opportunities for a life far beyond what she can offer him.

Six years after Anakin leaves Tatooine, Shmi falls in love with Cliegg Lars. Fortunately at the same time Watto has racked up huge debts and so agrees to sell Shmi to Cliegg. Her new owner immediately grants her freedom. They marry and Shmi becomes stepmother to Owen, a child she quickly comes to love and treat as her own son.

DID YOU KNOW?

Shmi is the one who gives C-3PO his first coverings, two years after Anakin leaves with Qui-Gon.

WATTO

The blue-skinned Watto is a former soldier from Toydaria who certainly lives up to his species' reputation for being stingy and bad-tempered. He owns a junk dealership in Mos Espa on Tatooine, from which he sells a wide range of machinery. Those who barter with him discover that he is a shrewd merchant and his greedy and immoral nature means he's always trying to get one over on those around him.

Watto also loves to gamble, which is how he comes into possession of the slaves Anakin and Shmi Skywalker, winning them in a bet. Anakin proves particularly useful to Watto due to his gift for mechanics and his affinity for Podracing, a sport Watto soon enters his young charge into. For Watto Podracing is a passion and an opportunity for some major gambling. He doesn't even show loyalty to his own entrant, as he often bets against Anakin. The Toydarian is certain Anakin cannot win the Boonta Eve Classic and so agrees to a bet where Qui-Gon gets Anakin if the boy wins the race, and if the boy loses Watto will receive the Jedi's Podracer (which is actually built by Anakin himself). Anakin wins the race and also his freedom. Unfortunately, Shmi is not freed at the same time, but Watto's obsession with gambling leads him to rack up such huge debts that he is eventually forced to sell her.

When his shop is running smoothly, Watto likes to fly up to the nest he's had built above the premises, which is reminiscent of the muck nests of Watto's native Toydaria. In the nest he keeps his treasured collection of Podrace memorabilia, which includes the Grand Trophy from Ando Prime Centrum's course and a victory chain stolen from the racer Sebulba.

DID YOU KNOW?

The Jedi can use mind tricks to convince many species to do their bidding, but Toydarians like Watto are immune from such ruses.

STAR WARS™
EPISODE II
ATTACK OF THE CLONES

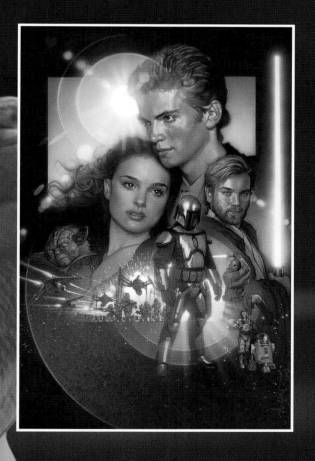

There is unrest in the Galactic Se
Several thousand solar systems
declared their intentions to leave
the Republic.

This separatist movement, under
leadership of themysterious Coun
Dooku, has made it difficult for t
limited number of Jedi Knights to
maintain peace and order in the g

Senator Amidala, the former Quee
of Naboo, is returning to the Gala
Senate to vote on the critical issu
of creating an army of the Republ
to assist the overwhelmed Jedi...

SENATOR PALPATINE

On the surface, Palpatine is an upstanding Naboo man who's risen through the ranks to become the planet's Senator to the Galactic Republic. Untainted by claims of corruption or greed, he is known for being patient, self-confident, and diligent; a man who is never afraid to speak his mind or to chastise those who abuse their power. Due to the respect he has built, he even becomes the Supreme Chancellor after Padmé Amidala puts forward a Vote of No Confidence in the previous incumbent.

Behind his virtuous public face, from a young age Palpatine has been a disciple of the dark side of the Force, rising as the evil Darth Sidious. Although the Sith have been hidden for a thousand years, Palpatine has bigger plans. He begins to use his considerable political skill to put in place a divide and conquer strategy, secretly orchestrating the invasion of Naboo and the Separatist movement, which eventually leads to the Clone Wars. Not suspected by those around him, Palpatine is able to consolidate power until he ultimately declares himself Emperor.

One of the major pieces of his plan is to destroy the Jedi. He ensures that the clone army is made completely subservient to his command so that when ordered, they do not hesitate to kill the very Jedi warriors who have fought alongside them. Not everything goes his way though, as he is hideously scarred during a battle with Jedi Master Mace Windu. Palpatine is so shrewd that he even uses this to his advantage. During the battle with Windu, he exploits the wounds the Jedi inflicts – as well as Windu's desire to summarily execute the newly declared Emperor – to convince Anakin Skywalker to join him. This completes the young Jedi's journey to the dark side.

DID YOU KNOW?

Palpatine was drawn to the dark side as a youth by a man publicly known as Hugo Demask, who was secretly the Sith Lord Darth Plagueis.

Yoda may be small, but he is renowned throughout the galaxy as one of the most skilled and powerful Jedi Masters. It's not just his abilities with a lightsaber and mastery of the Force that has amazed many over the years, but also how wise and skilful a negotiator he is. He has been a Jedi for over 800 years, and in that time he has travelled to hundreds of worlds in his quest to understand the true nature of the Force.

The green being has spent centuries training young Jedi and is known as a harsh but fair instructor. Yoda makes his students unlearn everything that they have been taught so that they can tune in to the world around them and learn the subtle truths of the Force. He tries to pass on to successive generations of Jedi students his belief that the Force should be used for knowledge, not for attack. The great Jedi Master also impresses the importance of being thoughtful and deliberate, and that careful contemplation is much better than rash action.

Yoda faces one of his greatest challenges when a split occurs in the galaxy and the Clone Wars erupt. He remains at the forefront of the Order as the Jedi turn from a stabilising force as peacekeepers to battlefield commanders. Although he's a proponent of peace, his skills with a lightsaber are recognised as the greatest in the galaxy. His diminutive stature should make it difficult for him to take on much larger opponents, but his shrewd mind and unparalleled ability to use the Force make him the ultimate Jedi warrior, both in one-on-one combat and when controlling the action on a battlefield.

Yoda is one of the few Jedi to survive the purge that almost obliterates the Jedi Order, going into exile on the swampy planet of Dagobah.

DID YOU KNOW?

Yoda has five toes, three on the front of his foot and two more towards the back.

R2-D2

R2-D2 (also known as Artoo-Detoo) is an astromech droid, a class of robots that are used as versatile utility droids, particularly handy for the maintenance and repair of starships. Hidden away in various panels on his body are a range of built-in tools, from welding torches to computer interfaces. Although his squat stature suggests he'd have problems with things like stairs, he's equipped with blasters that let him fly when necessary.

Like other astromech droids, he is designed to operate in deep space, interfacing with fighter craft and computer systems to augment the capabilities of the ships and their pilots. He monitors and diagnoses flight performance, maps and stores hyperspace data, and pinpoints technical errors or faulty computer coding. R2 speaks in a complex and very dense electronic language. This means that while he can understand most forms of human communication, his own speech needs to be translated by a ship's computer or an interpreter droid.

Built on the planet of Nubia, R2 is assigned to serve on Queen Padmé Amidala's Royal Starship during the Trade Federation's blockade of Naboo. This brings him into contact with the Jedi Obi-Wan Kenobi and Qui-Gon Jinn, as well as Anakin Skywalker. An excellent navigator, R2 assists Anakin as the boy destroys the droid army control ship, thereby helping to end the blockade. It is also around this time that he first meets the protocol droid C-3PO, which begins an enduring friendship and shared adventures in some of the most tumultuous events in the history of the galaxy.

DID YOU KNOW?

In the mid-1980s, R2-D2 and C-3PO got their own animated TV show, *Star Wars: Droids.*

C-3PO

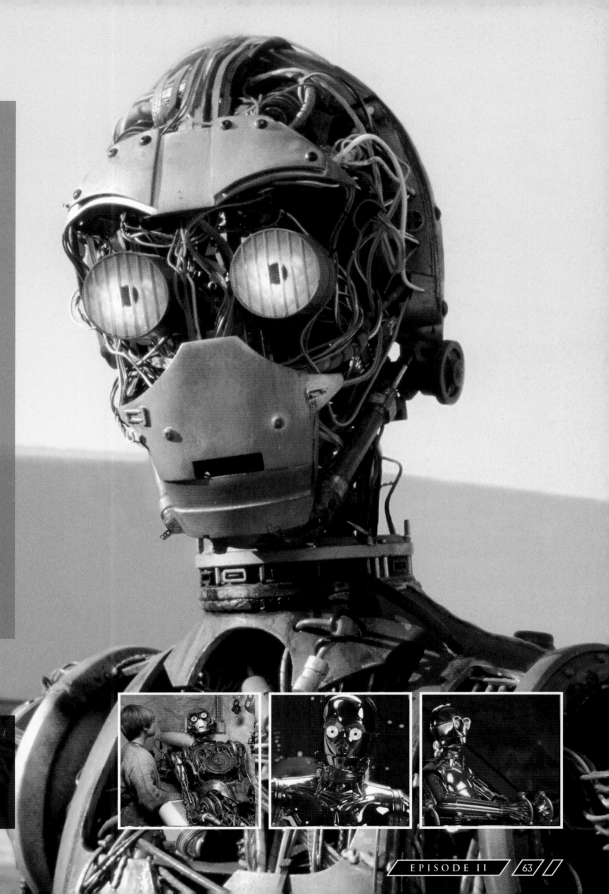

C-3PO was built by Anakin Skywalker on the planet Tatooine largely from parts the boy scavenged in Watto's junk shop. His main framework comes from an 80-year-old Cybot Galactica protocol droid that Anakin managed to repair, building many of the missing pieces himself. Anakin spent many hours working on the droid, putting him together so that his mother had something to help her with household chores.

Highly skilled and dedicated, Anakin programmed his machine with the detailed knowledge of over 5,000 droids. C-3PO also has a great gift for language, as he's conversant in over six million forms of communication. This skill is due to a TranLang III communications module, which Anakin scavenged from a broken droid that once belonged to his former owner, Gardulla the Hutt. Unfortunately for C-3PO, Anakin is unable to complete the droid before he leaves Tatooine. C-3PO is given new eyes shortly before the boy's departure, but at this time he has no 'skin', largely because droid plating is very expensive.

Initially left behind on Tatooine with Shmi Skywalker, he is reunited with Anakin shortly before the start of the Clone Wars. Around this time he meets the droid who will become his lifelong friend, R2-D2, which begins a relationship that will give them a pivotal role in the fate of the galaxy.

DID YOU KNOW?

Shmi Skywalker gives C-3PO his first grey and rust-coloured coverings, which are changed to silver when he becomes Padmé Amidala's protocol droid during the Clone Wars.

There was unrest in the Galactic Senate.

Several thousand solar systems had declared their intentions to leave the Republic. This movement, led by the mysterious Count Dooku, made it difficult for the limited number of Jedi Knights to maintain peace and order in the galaxy.

Padmé Amidala, formerly Queen of Naboo, now a Senator, returned to the Galactic Senate on Coruscant, in order to vote on the issue of creating an Army of the Republic to assist the overwhelmed Jedi.

A small group of dignitaries waited on the landing platform as Senator Amidala's cruiser landed, escorted by two Naboo fighter craft.

"We made it. I guess I was wrong, there was no danger," said a male fighter pilot to his female co-pilot.

The pair watched as the cruiser's ramp lowered and Senator Amidala walked out, accompanied by a handmaiden and four troopers. Suddenly a blinding flash and a huge explosion hurled the party to the ground.

As sirens blared and smoke swirled, the pilots ran towards the semi-conscious Senator, ripping off their helmets to better survey the devastation and revealing themselves as the real Padmé Amidala and her trusty head of security, Captain Typho.

Padmé bent over the fatally wounded woman on the ground. It was Cordé, her handmaiden and decoy.

"M'lady, so sorry… I failed you," croaked Cordé as her eyelids flickered and closed for the last time.

"Senator, You're still in danger here," urged Typho, as Padmé cradled the corpse of her loyal servant.

"I shouldn't have come back," wept Senator Padmé.

"This vote is very important. You did your duty, Cordé did hers. Now come!" Typho said, pulling Padmé inside.

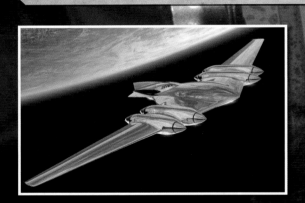

Later that day Chancellor Palpatine called the Jedi to his office.

"More and more star systems are joining the Separatists," Palpatine warned the Jedi. "I will not let this Republic that has stood for a thousand years be split in two. My negotiations will not fail."

"If they do, you must realise there are not enough Jedi to protect the Republic," replied Jedi Master Mace Windu. "We are keepers of the peace, not soldiers."

Palpatine turned to Yoda. "Do you think it will really come to war?" he asked.

Yoda closed his eyes. "The Dark Side clouds everything. Impossible to see, the future is," he murmured.

An aide announced the arrival of Senator Amidala. The assembled gathering stood to greet her.

"Senator Amidala," said Yoda. "Your tragedy on the landing platform…terrible. Seeing you alive brings warm feelings to my heart."

Padmé smiled, then immediately asked the Jedi if they had any idea who was behind the attempt on her life.

"Our intelligence points to disgruntled spice miners on the moons of Naboo," said Mace.

Padmé wasn't convinced. "I think Count Dooku was behind it," she said. The Jedi Knights looked at each other in surprise.

"He is a political idealist, not a murderer," said Ki-Adi-Mundi.

"Count Dooku was once a Jedi. He couldn't assassinate anyone. It's not in his character," added Mace.

But the Jedi had to agree that Padmé was in grave danger.

Palpatine turned to the Jedi Council. "May I suggest the Senator be placed under the protection of your graces," he said.

Padmé bristled. "Chancellor, if I may comment, I do not believe the situation is that serious?"

Palpatine interrupted. "No, but I do. The additional security might be disruptive for you, but perhaps someone you are familiar with. An old friend… like Master Kenobi?"

"That's possible," agreed Mace. "He has just returned from a border dispute on Ansion."

"Do it for me M'Lady," said Palpatine.

"The thought of losing you is unbearable."

Seeing Palpatine's grim expression, Padmé reluctantly agreed to accept the offer of Jedi security.

Later that evening Obi-Wan Kenobi and his Padawan learner Anakin Skywalker arrived on Coruscant.

As they made their way up to Senator Amidala's apartments in the Senate Building, Anakin fiddled nervously with his robes.

"I haven't felt you this tense since we fell into that nest of gundarks," Obi-Wan said.

"You fell into that nightmare, Master, and I rescued you, remember?" Anakin replied.

"Obi-Wan smiled. You're sweating Anakin. Relax. Take a deep breath."

But Anakin could not master his nerves.

"I… I haven't seen her in ten years, Master," he stammered.

An old friend waited to greet them in Amidala's apartment.

"Obi! Mesa soo smilen to be seein yousa," Jar Jar Binks said, rushing towards the Jedi and pumping their hands excitedly.

"Good to see you again, Jar Jar," smiled Obi-Wan.

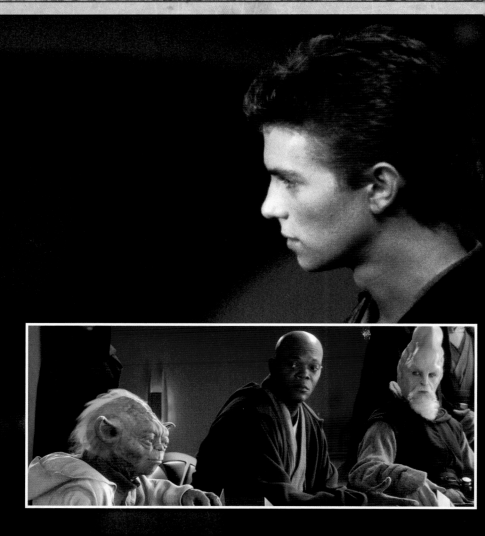

The Gungan showed the two Jedi out onto the balcony where Padmé was deep in conversation with Captain Typho and her handmaiden, Dormé.

"It's a great pleasure to see you again, M'Lady," said Obi-Wan as Padmé walked over and shook his hand.

"It has been far too long, Master Kenobi," she replied, before turning to greet his Jedi apprentice. "Ani?" her voice was incredulous as she stared at the young man she'd last seen ten years before. "My goodness, you've grown," she said.

"So have you, grown more beautiful, I mean well, for a Senator" Anakin stuttered.

Padmé laughed and shook her head. "Ani, you'll always be that little boy I knew on Tatooine."

The group moved towards the seating area and Captain Typho filled the Jedi in on the assassination attempt and present danger.

"I don't want extra security, I want to know who is trying to kill me," Padmé said with irritation. Obi-Wan frowned.

"We're here to protect you, Senator, not to start an investigation."

Anakin jumped to Padmé's defence. "We will find out who's trying to kill you Padmé," he promised defiantly.

Obi-Wan was furious at his apprentice's disobedience and a heated debate followed over the real aims of their mission.

"We will do exactly as the Council has instructed," Obi-Wan ordered. "And you will learn your place, young one," he added, silencing Anakin with a glare.

When night fell, two armour-clad bounty hunters met on the ledge of a skyscraper.

"I hit the ship, but they used a decoy," explained one - a woman.

"We'll have to try something more subtle this time, Zam," said the other, a stocky man. "My client is getting impatient." He handed Zam a tube full of centipede-like kouhuns. "Take these. Be careful. They're very poisonous," he instructed. "There can be no mistakes this time."

Taking the tube full of deadly creatures, Zam jumped onto her hovering speeder and zoomed off into the night.

While Padmé Amidala slept peacefully in the bedroom of her apartment, her Jedi protectors paced the floor of her living room.

"Captain Typho has more than enough men downstairs. No assassin will try that way. Any activity up here?" Obi-Wan asked Anakin.

"Quiet as a tomb. But I don't like waiting for something to happen to her," replied Anakin.

Obi-Wan pulled a view scanner from his utility belt. "What is she thinking?" he tutted, seeing the darkened screen.

"She covered the cameras. I don't think she liked me watching her," explained Anakin. "But she

programmed R2-D2 to warn us of intruders, we want to catch the assassin, don't we, Master?"

Obi-Wan paused. "You're using her as bait!" he exclaimed.

"It was her idea" said Anakin. "Don't worry; I can sense everything going on in that room. Trust me."

Obi-Wan was not reassured. "It's too risky, besides, your senses aren't that attuned, my young apprentice."

"And yours are?" sniped Anakin.

While the Jedi Master and apprentice bickered, a probe droid carrying the deadly kouhuns hovered outside Padmé's bedroom window.

Stealthily, it shut down the security system then cut a small hole in the glass.

Removing the glass it attached a tube to the window. Two kouhuns crawled through in through the blinds and headed down the wall and across the carpet to the Senator's bed.

R2-D2 bleeped, scanned the room, and then shut down without having detected the scuttling creatures.

Next door Obi-Wan had remarked on Anakin's general fatigue and the apprentice admitted his sleep was disturbed by nightmares about his mother.

"I'd much rather dream about Padmé. Just being around her again is intoxicating," he told Obi-Wan.

Obi-Wan was not impressed by this confession of affection. "Be mindful of your thoughts, they betray you," he told Anakin. "You've made a commitment to the Jedi Order. And don't forget, she's a politician. They're not to be trusted."

Anakin laughed this off but Obi-Wan continued with his diatribe.

"It is my experience that Senators are only focused on pleasing those who fund their campaigns and are happy to forget democracy in order to get those funds."

"Not another lecture," groaned Anakin.

"Besides you're generalizing. Chancellor Palpatine doesn't appear to be corrupt."

"I have observed that he is very clever in following the passions and prejudices of the Senators," said Obi-Wan.

"I think he's a good man…" Anakin began. He suddenly broke off, clutched his lightsaber and rushed suddenly for the door to Padmé's bedroom.

"I felt it too," cried Obi-Wan drawing his weapon and following. The pair arrived in time to see the poisonous kouhuns crawling inches from Padmé's face.

With one stroke of his lightsaber Anakin killed them. Padmé awoke with a start and gasped as she took in the scene and realised how close she'd been to death. Sensing a presence at the window, Obi-Wan leapt at the glass, crashed through and grabbed the hovering probe droid with both hands. It whizzed off at high speed, with Obi-Wan clinging on.

"Stay here!" Anakin told Padmé. He rushed out of the building, vaulted into the cockpit of a nearby speeder and took off, gunning the craft towards the lines of speeder traffic above.

Up ahead the droid raced at oncoming vehicles, bashing into buildings in an attempt to dislodge its heavy hitchhiker. It headed for a speeder parked in the hidden alcove of a building. Bounty hunter Zam Wesell watched the droid approach, pulled out a long rifle and blasted it, sending Obi-Wan plummeting fifty stories towards the ground. Just in time Anakin spotted his falling mentor and sped beneath him to halt his fall. With a puff and a grunt Obi-Wan landed on the nose of Anakin's speeder and climbed into the passenger seat.

"What took you so long?" he grunted, trying to catch his breath.

"Sorry Master, I couldn't find a speeder that I liked," Anakin replied, intentionally trying to irk his mentor. He drove kamikaze-style after Zam's fleeing speeder, treating Obi-Wan to a white-knuckle ride.

"Sorry Master, I forgot you don't like flying" Anakin grinned, seeing Obi-Wan grimace as they sped vertically towards the ground.

"I don't mind flying but what you're doing is suicide," gasped Obi-Wan. The pair chased the bounty hunter through a power refinery. Zam's speeder ducked into a tunnel and inexplicably Anakin seemed to give up the chase, pointing his speeder in a totally different direction.

"What are you doing?" Obi-Wan yelled. "He went that way!"

"It's a short cut," smiled Anakin. Then without warning he leapt out of thedriver's set and dropped from the speeder.

"I hate it when he does that," groaned Obi-Wan seizing the speeder controls and diving after him.

Anakin landed splat on the nose of Zam's speeder. He tried his best to disable it with his lightsaber but the weapon flew out of his hands. Luckily, Obi-Wan, flying nearby, used the Force to attract Anakin's falling lightsaber. After a lengthy tussle Anakin managed to grab Zam's weapon. Still, things didn't quite go according to plan. The gun went off, blowing a hole in the speeder which careered wildly out of control dropping from the sky onto the street below. Anakin was flung onto the pavement and before he could pick

himself up, Zam fled into the nearest club. Landing close by Obi-Wan handed Anakin his lightsaber. He warned him not to lose it again. "Why do I get the feeling you're going to be the death of me?" he told Anakin.

"Don't say that, Master. You're the closest thing I have to a father," Anakin replied.

"Then why don't you listen to me?" Obi-Wan protested.

"I am trying," said Anakin, surveying the low-lifes in the club.

Obi-Wan walked towards the bar to get a drink.

Suddenly he sensed movement behind him. He turned just in time to see Zam aiming her gun at his back. In a flash Obi-Wan had disabled her with his lightsaber and the two Jedi man-handled her outside.

"Who hired you?" Obi-Wan shouted as they pinned Zam down.

"A bounty hunter called…" Wham! A toxic dart shot into Zam's neck. With a surprised blink she died turning instantly back into her alien Clawdite form. She'd been a changeling. Obi-Wan and Anakin looked up just in time to see the armoured assassin taking off from a roof above.

The next day Obi-Wan and Anakin received a new set of orders from Yoda and the council.

"Track down this bounty hunter, you must, Obi-Wan," said Yoda.

"Find out who he's working for," added Mace. He turned to Anakin. "Escort the Senator back to her home planet of Naboo. Travel as refugees."

Predictably, Padmé took some convincing, but Anakin enlisted Palpatine to help him persuade her that this was the safest course of action.

"So, they have finally given you an assignment. Your patience has paid off," the chancellor told Anakin.

"Your guidance more than my patience," replied Anakin.

"You don't need guidance, Anakin," said Palpatine. "Learn to trust your feelings. Then you will be invincible. I see you becoming the greatest of all the Jedi. Even more powerful than Master Yoda."

In the Jedi Temple Mace Windu, Obi-Wan and Yoda were also discussing Anakin's prowess and promise.

"I'm concerned for my Padawan. He is not ready to be given this assignment on his own," said Obi-Wan.

"The Council is confident in its decision," argued Yoda.

"Remember, Obi-Wan," Mace chided. "If the prophecy is true, your apprentice is the only one who can bring the Force back into balance."

Padmé was in her apartments packing. She gave an honoured Jar Jar the responsibility of taking her place in the Senate during her extended leave of absence. Then she turned to Anakin.

"I do not like this idea of hiding," she told him.

"Don't worry, now that the Council has ordered an investigation, it won't take Master Obi-Wan long to find this bounty hunter," Anakin said. "Sometimes we must let go of our pride and do what is requested of us."

"You've grown up," Padmé murmured, impressed.

Anakin told Padmé how stifled he felt by the fact that Obi-Wan could not recognise the fact he was no longer a child.

"I'm ready for the trials, but he won't let me move on," he moaned.

"Don't try to grow up too fast," warned Padmé.

"I am grown up. You said it yourself," he breathed, looking deep into her eyes.

"Please don't look at me like that," she said, returning to her packing. "It makes me feel uncomfortable."

"Sorry, M'Lady," Anakin said, leaving her to finish her packing.

When Padmé's suitcases were full, she dressed in peasant's robes and travelled to the spaceport freighter docks accompanied by Captain Typho and Dormé, to meet Obi-Wan and Anakin. They said their goodbyes

and Obi-Wan assured Padmé he'd get to the bottom of the assassination plot quickly so that she could return.

"May the Force be with you," he told Anakin, placing paternal hands on his shoulders.

"Suddenly, I'm afraid," Padmé said as she and Anakin walked towards a giant starfreighter.

"I am too," admitted Anakin. "But don't worry. We have Artoo with us."

Padmé giggled.

After seeing Anakin and Padmé off, Obi-Wan walked downtown to a scruffy looking restaurant called Dex's Diner. He took a seat and waited for the droid waitress to announce his arrival. A huge head poked through the kitchen hatch.

"Obi-Wan!" said Dexter Jettster delightedly, dragging his bald, sweaty, alien form over to Obi-Wan's booth. "So, my friend. What can I do for ya?"

Obi-Wan showed him the toxic dart that had killed the bounty hunter. Dexter picked it up delicately between puffy fingers and peered at it. "What you got here is a Kamino saber dart," he said.

"I'm not familiar with Kamino. Is it in the Republic?" asked Obi-Wan.

"It's beyond the Outer Rim. About twelve parsecs outside the Rishi Maze. Kaminoans are cloners. Damned good ones, too."

"Are they friendly?" asked Obi-Wan.

"Depends on how good your manners are, and how big your pocket book is" laughed Dex.

But, after hours of research in the Jedi Temple Archives, Obi-Wan could find no trace of Kamino. He called the librarian but she could not help.

"If an item does not appear in our records, it does not exist," she told him.

A perplexed Obi-Wan went straight to Yoda who was teaching a class of Jedi younglings.

"Lost a planet, Master Obi-Wan has. How embarrassing! Gather around the map reader, clear your minds and find Obi-Wan's wayward planet, we will," Yoda instructed. The children did as they were told.

"Gravity's silhouette remains, but the star and all the planets, disappeared, they have," said Yoda. "How can this be?"
A small child piped up. "Because someone erased it from the archive memory."

Obi-Wan stared; Yoda chuckled.

"Truly wonderful, the mind of a child is. The Padawan is right. Go to the centre of gravity's pull and find your planet you will," he told Obi-Wan, adding, "only a Jedi could have erased those files. But who and why is harder to answer."

En route to Naboo, Padmé and Anakin had time for a heart to heart.

"Must be difficult having sworn your life to the Jedi, not being able to visit the places you like…"

"Or be with the people that I love," Anakin added.

"Love?" Padmé asked, "I thought that was forbidden for a Jedi."

"Attachment is forbidden," he said. "Possession is forbidden. Compassion, which I would define as unconditional love, is central to a Jedi's life, you might say we are encouraged to love." Padmé stared at him in wonder, she realised how he had changed and grown.

"You haven't changed a bit," said Anakin seriously. "You're exactly the way I remember you in my dreams."

The pair fell into embarrassed silence. Their first appointment on Naboo was with the new Queen Jamillia. She received them in the throne room and Padmé filled her in on the precarious situation.

"If the Senate votes to create an army, I'm sure it's going to push us into civil war," Padmé told her.

"Do you see any way, through negotiations, to bring the Separatists back into the Republic?" asked the Queen.

"Not if they feel threatened," said Padmé. "My guess is they'll turn to the Trade Federation." There were grunts of displeasure from those who remembered the Trade Federation's blockade and invasion of Naboo a decade ago.

"It's outrageous, that after the hearings and trials Nute Gunray is still the Viceroy of the Trade Federation," said Sio Bibble, aide to the Queen.

"We must keep our faith in the Republic. The day we stop believing democracy can work is the day we lose it," said Queen Jamillia wisely.

She asked what Padmé's plans were. Anakin bristled as Padmé explained she wanted to head to the isolated Lake Country.

"Excuse me!" he sniffed. "I'm in charge of security here."

"And this is my home," snapped Padmé. "I know it well. I think it would be wise to use my knowledge in this instance."

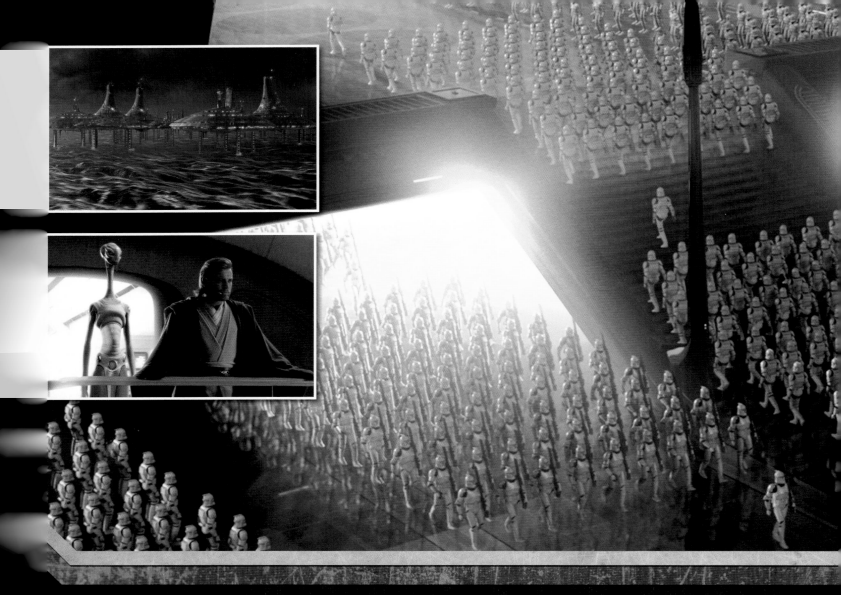

While Padmé and Anakin were finding their feet on Naboo, Obi-Wan was on his way to Kamino which, despite its absence from all maps, was right where it was supposed to be.

He landed in Tipoca – an ultra-modern city resting on stilts above the raging seas of this watery planet. Obi-Wan ran through driving rain to a tower on the far side of the platform and was greeted by a willowy, white alien with a long neck.

"Master Jedi, the Prime Minister is expecting you," Taun We told Obi-Wan.

"I'm expected?" Obi-Wan asked warily.

"Of course! After all these years, we were beginning to think you weren't coming," she said, leading him down a bright corridor to Lama Su's office.

"I trust you are going to enjoy your stay," began Lama Su, gesturing Obi-Wan to a chair. "And now to business. You will be delighted to hear we are on schedule. Two hundred thousand units are ready, with a million more on the way."

"That's… good news," Obi-Wan replied, improvising, for he had no idea what the Lama Su was telling him.

"Please tell your Master Sifo-Dyas his order will be met on time."

Obi-Wan was shocked. He had no choice but to tell Lama Su that Sifo-Dyas had been dead for almost a decade.

"I'm so sorry to hear that," remarked Lama Su. "I'm sure he'd have been proud of the army of clones we've built for him."

"When my Master first contacted you about the army, did he say who it was for?" asked Obi-Wan.

"Of course. This army is for the Republic," smiled the Prime Minister, rising and leading Obi-Wan towards the door.

"Come. Of course you must be anxious to inspect it."

Anakin had never seen anywhere more beautiful than the mountain-ringed lake retreat on Naboo where he now found himself with Padmé. She explained that as a child she used to visit for school trips. We used to swim to that island, lie on the sand and let the sun dry us."

"I don't like sand," said Anakin, recalling his childhood on the desert planet Tatooine. "It's coarse and rough and irritating and it gets everywhere."

He moved towards Padmé and touched her arm, stroking the skin. "Not like here," he continued. "Here, everything's soft and smooth."

They were so close now that he bent to kiss her.
"No," said Padmé, pulling away.
"I shouldn't have done that." Anakin realised.
"I'm sorry," he said.

Obi-Wan's tour of the clone centre began with a look into a classroom. It was filled with identical young boys.

"This group was created about five years ago," said Lama Su, explaining to the Jedi Knight that they used growth acceleration process to ensure the clones matured quickly. The next room held hundreds of older clones, all aged about 20.

"They take any order without question. We modified their genetic structure to make them less independent than the original host," said Lama Su.

"Who was that?" asked Obi-Wan.

"A bounty hunter called Jango Fett," replied Lama Su. "We keep him here." Lama Su told Obi-Wan that Fett had demanded one unaltered clone for himself – a pure genetic replication without tampering.

"I would like to meet this Jango Fett," said Obi-Wan, looking down from the balcony of the room they'd just entered. Below was a parade ground where thousands of clone troopers were drilling. The clone army was indeed impressive.

After the tour Taun We took Obi-Wan to Jango's apartment.

"Boba, is your father here?" Taun We asked the small boy who answered the door. He was identical to the many young clones they'd seen. Boba Fett stepped aside to allow Taun We and Obi-Wan entry. Jango Fett was inside. He was a mean-looking, stocky man with a face pitted with scars.

"Jango, welcome back. Was your trip productive?" Taun We asked.

"Fairly," grunted Jango, sizing up Obi-Wan.

"This is Jedi Master Obi-Wan Kenobi," come to check on our progress,"Taun We said.

"Your clones are very impressive, you must be proud," Obi-Wan told Jango. He tried to ask whether Jango's recent journeys involved a trip to Coruscant but Jango would not give a straight answer. Neither did he appear to know Sifo-Dyas. He claimed instead to have been recruited by a man called Tyranus on one of the moons of Bogden. When Obi-Wan took his leave Jango bid him a civil farewell.

"Always a pleasure to meet a Jedi," he growled.

As soon as he closed the door, he turned to Boba.

"Pack your things," he told his son. "We're leaving."

On Naboo Padmé and Anakin were flirting. He asked her about past loves and she told him she'd had a crush, aged 12, on a boy named Palo.

"I went into public service. He went on to become an artist," she told Anakin.

"Maybe he was the smart one," replied Anakin.

"You really don't like politicians, do you?" she said.

"I like two or three, but I'm not really sure about one

of them," he smiled, jumping on a grazing shaak's back and attempting to ride it. The shaak bucked him off and he pretended to be hurt.

Padmé ran to Anakin and he grabbed her so that they rolled over and over in the long grass.

While they dined together that evening Anakin amused Padmé by using the Force to summon fruit from her plate to his. Cutting it delicately he sent it floating back slice by slice into her waiting mouth.

"If Master Obi-Wan caught me doing this, he'd be very grumpy," he smiled.

As the days passed Anakin grew bolder. One night he opened his heart.

"From the moment I met you, not a day has gone by when I haven't thought of you. The closer I get to you, the worse it gets. The thought of not being with you… I can't breathe. You are in my very soul, tormenting me…" Padmé met Anakin's gaze, then looked away.

"If you are suffering as much as I am, please tell me," he continued.

"Listen. We live in a real world," she urged. "Come back to it. You're studying to be a Jedi. I'm a Senator.

If you follow your thoughts through to conclusion, it'll take us to a place we cannot go…regardless of the way we feel about each other." Anakin's eyes lit up. "Then you do feel something!" he cried.

"I will not give in to this," she said.

He tried to persuade her that they could keep their liaison a secret but she was horrified by the idea of living a lie.

"You're right," he agreed reluctantly. "It would destroy us."

On Kamino, Obi-Wan said good-bye to Lama Su and Taun We and headed to the landing platform.

"Tell your Council the first battalions are ready. Remind them, if they need more troops, it will take more time to grow them," said Lama Su.

Obi-Wan nodded and headed out of the tower into the storm. He waited until he was alone and then walked to his starfighter. "Arfour, scramble code five" he told his droid.

R4 beeped and whistled, transmitting a coded message to Yoda and Mace Windu back on Coruscant.

"I have successfully made contact with the Prime Minister of Kamino," his hologram told the Jedi. "They are using a bounty hunter named Jango Fett to create a clone army. I have a feeling he is the assassin we're looking for."

Mace Windu asked Obi-Wan if the cloners were involved in the assassination plot, but Obi-Wan shook his head. He told Yoda and Mace that the cloners claimed Sifo-Dyas placed the order at the request of the Senate almost ten years ago.

"Whoever placed that order did not have the authorization of the Jedi Council," said Mace.

"Bring him here. Question him, we will," said Yoda.

As Obi-Wan's hologram faded Yoda turned to Mace.

"Blind we are, if creation of this clone army, we could not see," he said.

"I think it's time to inform the Senate our ability to use the Force has diminished," said Mace.

"Only the Dark Lord of the Sith knows of our weakness. If informed the Senate is, multiply our adversaries will," said Yoda sagely.

It didn't take Obi-Wan long to realise that Jango Fett was not going to wait around to be pulled in for questioning. On a neighbouring landing platform the bounty hunter and his son prepared to board their ship.

"Boba, get on board," yelled Jango, seeing Obi-Wan charging towards them.
Jango drew his gun and fired at Obi-Wan who drew his lightsaber and deflected the blast. Jango, in full armour, launched himself up and over Obi-Wan, landing on top of a nearby tower. He fired shot after shot, finishing with an explosive which blasted Obi-Wan off his feet. Obi-Wan's lightsaber skidded across the wet surface of the platform. In the cockpit of

Jango's ship, Boba grabbed the laser gun controls and began firing at Obi-Wan. Jango launched himself onto the Jedi and the pair began to fight. Jango launched a wire from his jet pack which caught around Obi-Wan but as they brawled the pair began asliding to the edge of the platform. Jango spiked the forearm claws of his suit into the surface to prevent himself slipping over into the violent waves, but Obi-Wan plummeted over the edge. For a few seconds they hung there.

"This is not good," Obi-Wan mutteredto himself, desperately trying to formulate a plan. He knew that eventually his weight would pull Jango over and they would both fall into the ocean. Jango ejected the wire

free from his wrist sending Obi-Wan falling towards the waves but with one massive effort Obi-Wan used the Force to wrap the flapping end of the wire round a pole halting his descent.

The Jedi pulled himself back up to safety, but he was too late to prevent Jango from jumping on to the spacecraft as Boba brought its engines to life. The ship rocketed into the air, but with lightning reflexes Obi-Wan removed a small tracking device from his belt and threw it onto the hull of the ship, where it stuck with a metallic clang.

Jango had escaped for now, but at least Obi-Wan could follow.

Despite the tranquil beauty of the lake retreat, Anakin was still plagued with nightmares about his mother. Following another restless night he tried meditating on the balcony. Even with his eyes closed he could sense Padmé behind him.

"Don't go, your presence is soothing," he told her.

"You had another nightmare," she said gently.

"I saw my mother. She is suffering, Padmé. She is in pain! I know I'm disobeying my mandate to protect you, Senator, but I have to go and help her," Anakin said.

Padmé's reply was instant. "I'll go with you," she said.

They took a starship to the outskirts of Mos Espa.

It was the first time Anakin had been back to Tatooine since the day Jedi Master Qui-Gon Jinn had freed him from slavery. Now he sought his old owner, Watto. Anakin and Padmé found the flying alien in front of his shop, tinkering with a droid.

"Let me help you with that," Anakin said in perfect Huttese, reaching out and taking the fiddly piece of equipment.

"What do you want? Wait! You're a Jedi! Whatever it is, I didn't do it," grunted Watto, dropping his screwdriver and cursing loudly.

"I'm looking for Shmi Skywalker," Anakin said, handing back the now-functioning droid. Realisation

dawned on Watto's face. Little Ani, the boy who could fix anything, had returned.

"It is you! You sure sprouted! A Jedi, whaddya know!" Watto cried.

But Anakin was not in the mood for emotional reunions.

"My mother?" he asked.

Watto told him that he had sold Shmi to a moisture farmer named Lars who lived on the other side of Mos Eisley. There was some good news though. According to the alien, Lars had freed Shmi and married her. There was no time to waste. Anakin and Padmé set off to find Lars.

Meanwhile, in deep space Obi-Wan was hard on the tail of the fleeing Jango Fett and his son. The pair did their best to lose him in an asteroid field. They deployed seismic chargers which blasted dangerous chunks from the asteroids, causing an interstellar obstacle course for Obi-Wan. But their skills were no match for the Jedi. He outwitted them by appearing to crash into a large asteroid and explode. In fact he'd created decoy explosions with spare part canisters and was taking cover in a blasted-out area on the pitted back side of the rock.

"We won't be seeing him again," laughed Jango, emerging from the asteroid belt and heading down toward the planet of Geonosis. Obi-Wan waited, then followed. He landed in the midst of a landscape of red rock, punctured only by tall stalagmites and large fleets of Trade Federation ships. What were they doing here? Checking his bearings Obi-Wan headed off into the night.

On Tatooine, Anakin and Padmé had at last located Lars' moisture farm. Walking towards the homestead they encountered a familiar face. It was the protocol droid Anakin had been making before Qui-Gon released him from servitude.

"Bless my circuits!" said C-3PO. "I'm so pleased to see you both!" The robot took them into a courtyard. There they found a young man and his girlfriend.

"I'm Owen Lars. This is my girlfriend, Beru," said the man. "I guess I'm your step-brother. I had a feeling you might show up some day."

"Is my mother here?" Anakin asked.

"No she's not!" The voice came from a frail, bearded man on a floating chair. One of his legs was missing, the other bandaged, but he held out his hand to Anakin.

"Cliegg Lars," he said. "Shmi is my wife, We should go inside. We have a lot to talk about."

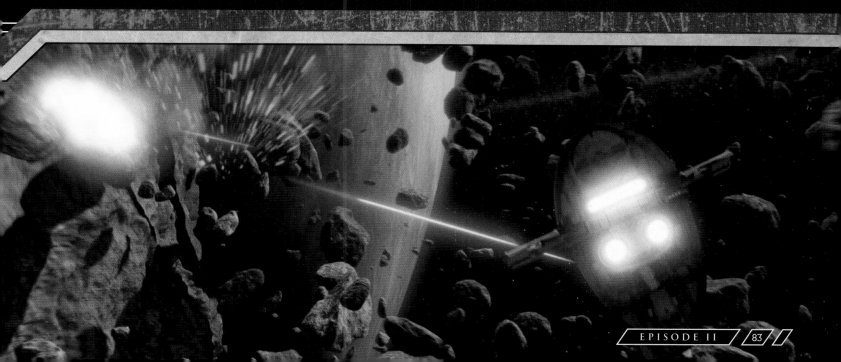

Inside the house Cliegg offered refreshments and told Anakin the tragic tale of his mother's fate.

"Your mother had gone out early, to pick mushrooms that grow on the vaporators. She was about halfway home when they took her. Those Tuskens walk like men, but they're vicious, mindless monsters. Thirty of us went out after her. Four returned. I'd be out there still, but...after I lost my leg I just couldn't ride any more," Cliegg grimaced, rubbing his throbbing stump. "I don't want to give up on her, but she's been gone a month. There's little hope she's lasted this long."

The Padawan could bear it no longer. He stood up.

"Where are you going?" Owen asked, as Anakin strode towards the door.

"To find my mother," Anakin answered.

"She's dead, son. Accept it," croaked Cliegg, but Anakin was already out in the desert. Padmé followed him but he told her to stay put.

"These are good people," he said. "You'll be safe here."

The Senator threw her arms around the Jedi and hugged him tightly.

"I won't be long," he promised, zooming off on Owen's speeder bike.

On Geonosis Obi-Wan made his way along a narrow, pillared corridor. Looking into a vent shaft he saw a huge underground facility where machines were busy constructing legions of battle droids, which passed by on conveyor belts. Voices in the corridor made him pause and he flattened himself to the wall. The source of the voices walked into view. Count Dooku was deep in conversation with Nute Gunray and other dignitaries.

"We must persuade the Commerce Guild and the Corporate Alliance to sign the treaty," Dooku said.

"What about the Senator from Naboo? Is she dead yet?" asked Nute. "I am not signing your treaty until I have her head on my desk."

"I am a man of my word, Viceroy," replied Dooku, coldly.

The party passed out of earshot and into a conference room. Obi-Wan sneaked behind them, stopping in an archway so he could hear what was said, unobserved.

Count Dooku sat at the head of the table. Jango Fett stood behind his chair. Clearing his throat Dooku addressed three opposition Senators, a Commerce Guild dignitary and a member of the Intergalactic Bank Clan.

"I am quite convinced that ten thousand more star systems will rally to our cause with your support," Dooku told them.

Shu Mai of the Commerce Guild looked worried. "What you are proposing could be construed as treason."

"The Techno Union army is at your disposal, Count" piped up Union rep Wat Tambor.

"And the Banking Clan will sign your treaty," said San Hill, the banker.

Dooku looked pleased. He gestured to Nute. "Our friends from the Trade Federation have pledged their support. And when their battle droids are combined with yours, we shall have an army greater than any in the galaxy. The Jedi will be overwhelmed and the Republic will agree to any demands we make."

Hiding, Obi-Wan's jaw dropped.

After hours of searching, Anakin at last located the Tusken camp. He crept towards the centre, working his way from hut to hut, catching snatches of Tusken conversation until he arrived at a hut with two guards. He wriggled round the back then took out his lightsaber and cut a hole in the wall. Carefully, he climbed through. Even after weeks of vivid nightmares about his mother, nothing could have prepared him for the sight of Shmi, beaten senseless and tied upright to a wooden frame.

He rushed to her, cut her free and gathered her broken body in his arms.

"Mum," he breathed.

Shmi opened her swollen eyelids. "Ani? Is it you?" she whispered.

"I'm here, you're safe," he told her.

"You look so handsome, my grown up son. I'm so proud of you," she said.

"I missed you," he told her, hugging her tightly. But Shmi's breaths were already becoming more shallow and irregular.

"Now I am complete. I love…" she began, before death claimed her.

Anakin sat on the floor of the Tusken hut, cradling his dead mother in his arms until the pale light grew, indicating dawn. Suddenly he lifted his head.

The two guards had no idea what was coming. Before they could turn to check out his footsteps, they were floored by Anakin's lightsaber. His face an ugly mask of rage and revenge, Anakin made his way further into camp.

Thousands of miles away in the Jedi Temple on Coruscant, Yoda closed his eyes.

"What is it?" asked Mace.

"Pain. Suffering. Death, I feel. Something terrible has happened. Young Skywalker is in pain. Terrible pain," said Yoda.

Horrified by what he had overheard between Dooku and the rest of the dignitaries, Obi-Wan returned to his ship. He needed to report his

news to Yoda, and fast.

"The transmitter is working, but we're not receiving a return signal," he told R4. "Corsucant's too far. Can you boost the power?" R4 beeped a negative.

"Maybe we can contact Anakin on Naboo. It's much closer," he said, jumping into the cockpit and trying to reach Anakin. There was no reply so Obi-Wan located Anakin's tracking signal. "That's him all right. But it's

coming from Tatooine. What the blazes is he doing there? I told him to stay on Naboo," the unflappable Jedi's tone was angry. "Anakin, my long range transmitter has been knocked out. Retransmit this message to Coruscant," he tried again.

In the cockpit of Anakin and Padmé's ship, R2 beeped as he received the message. He listened dutifully to Obi-Wan's desperate plea which suddenly cut out.

Meanwhile Anakin remained unaware of the latest worrying developments in the Separatist's plot. He arrived back at the homestead mid-morning, Shmi's body wrapped and tied to his speeder. Wordlessly he greeted Padmé and Cliegg and carried his mother into the house.

"Are you hungry?" Padmé asked him later as he stood at a workbench, repairing a part from the speeder bike. He didn't reply so she placed the tray of food next to him.

"Life seems so much simpler when you're fixing things," Anakin said quietly. "I'm good at fixing things, always was. But I couldn't," he broke off, tears clouding his eyes. "Why'd she have to die? Why couldn't I save her? I know I could have!" Words failed him.

"Sometimes there are things no one can fix. You're not all-powerful, Ani," Padmé tried.

Anakin turned towards her angrily.

"Well I should be. Someday I will be the most powerful Jedi ever! I will even learn to stop people from dying."

Padmé attempted to calm him.

"It's all Obi-Wan's fault! He's jealous! He's holding me back!" he yelled, hurling his wrench across the room.

Padmé stared in shock.

"I killed them all," he said, focusing on her suddenly as if he'd just returned from a dark, distant place. "Not just the male Tuskens, but the women and children too. They're like animals and I slaughtered them like animals! I hate them!"

Slowly he lowered himself to the floor, weeping for his loss and his terrible actions.

Padmé knelt beside him. "To be angry is to be human," she soothed.

"No, I'm a Jedi. I'm better than this," he said as she rocked and caressed him.

That night Anakin buried his mother on Cliegg Lars' farm.

"I wasn't strong enough to save you, Mum," he said, throwing sand on her grave, "but I promise I won't fail again."

A beeping sound brought him back to the here and now. R2 had brought Obi-Wan's message.

Anakin and Padmé returned to their ship and retransmitted Obi-Wan's message to Yoda and the Council. In it he recounted that he had tracked Jango Fett to the droid foundries on Geonosis. The Trade Federation was to take delivery of a droid army and none other than Nute Gunray was behind the assassination attempts on Senator Padmé Amidala.

"The Commerce Guilds and Coroporate Alliance have both pledged their armies to Count Dooku," continued Obi-Wan's voice "and are forming an... Wait!!

The message cut off. It seemed that Obi-Wan had been discovered and captured.

"More happening on Geonosis, I feel, than has been revealed," said Yoda.

"I agree," said Mace. He sent a hologram to Anakin and Padmé. "We will deal with Count Dooku. The most important thing for you is to stay where you are. Protect the Senator at all costs. That is your first priority," he told Anakin.

"Understood," said Anakin. The hologram switched off. Padmé checked the readout on the ship's control panel.

"They'll never get there in time to save him.

Look, Geonosis is less than a parsec away," she said, turning to Anakin who was lost in thought. "Ani, are you just going to sit here and let him die? He's your friend, your mentor," she continued frantically hitting buttons and flicking switches.

"He's like my father, but you heard Master Windu. He gave me strict orders to stay here."

"He gave you strict orders to protect me and I'm going to help Obi-Wan," yelled Padmé, over the noise of the ship's engines. "If you plan to protect me, you'll just have to come along."

Grinning, Anakin took the controls and manoeuvred the ship into space.

Chancellor Palpatine's office was full of worried Senators.

"The Commerce Guilds are preparing for war." said Bail Organa.

"Dooku must have made a treaty with them," mused Palpatine.

"The debate is over! Now we need that clone army," said Ask Aak.

"But the Senate will never approve the use of clones before the Separatists attack," replied Bail.

"This is a crisis! The Senate must vote the Chancellor emergency powers so he can approve the creation of an army!" said Mas Amedda.

"What Senator would have the courage to propose such a radical amendment?" asked Palpatine.

"If only Senator Amidala were here." said Mas.

Later that day the Senate came to order.

"In response to this direct threat to the Republic, mesa propose the Senate give immediately emergency powers to the Supreme Chancellor," said Jar Jar Binks from his floating pod.

There was mass applause. Then Palpatine spoke.

"It is with great reluctance that I have agreed to this calling. I love democracy and the Republic. The power you give me I will lay down when this crisis has abated. And as my first act with this new authority, I will create a grand army of the Republic to counter increasing threats from the Separatists."

Mace Windu and Yoda met in the main senate chamber later that day. They agreed that Mace would take all remaining Jedi and go to Geonosis to Obi-Wan's aid, while Yoda will visit the cloners on Kamino and see the army created for the Republic.

Obi-Wan was indeed in trouble. Droidekas had surrounded him while he was attempting to send his message to Anakin and the Jedi Council. They hadn't killed him, but had taken him captive. He found himself in a dark cell, suspended by a Force field and restrained by electric bolts which zapped him if he moved a muscle.

"Traitor," he cried as Count Dooku appeared at his side.

"My friend! This is a terrible mistake. They've gone too far," said the Count.

"I thought you were the leader here, Dooku," snarled Obi-Wan.

Dooku denied all involvement, saying he'd petition to have Obi-Wan released immediately.

"I hope it doesn't take too long. I have work to do," replied Obi-Wan. Dooku asked what Obi-Wan was doing on Geonosis and he told him he was tracking down Jango Fett. Again Dooku feigned ignorance.

"There are no bounty hunters here, the Geonosians don't trust them," he lied. Then his tone changed. "It's a great pity our paths have never crossed before, Obi-Wan," he said. "Qui-Gon spoke very highly of you. I wish he were still alive. I could use his help right now."

At the mention of his former Master's name Obi-Wan wrenched against his restraints, receiving shocks for his efforts. "Qui-Gon would never join you," he cried.

"You forget he was once my apprentice just as you were once his," said Dooku. "Qui-Gon knew about the corruption in the Senate, but he would never have gone along with it if he had known the truth. The Republic is now under the control of the Dark Lord of the Sith." Obi-Wan refused to believe this. "The Jedi would be aware of it!" he exclaimed.

"The dark side of the Force has clouded their vision, my friend," said Dooku. "Hundreds of Senators are now under the influence of Darth Sidious. The Viceroy of the Trade Federation was once in league with Sidious but he was betrayed ten years ago by the Dark Lord and came to me for help. You must join me, Obi-Wan. Together we'll destroy the Sith!"

"Never!" Obi-Wan shook his head as Dooku strode out of the cell. Clearly no release was imminent.

Some miles from Obi-Wan's prison, Anakin was piloting his ship to the ground, weaving around towering rock formations.

"Look, whatever happens out there, follow my lead," Padmé ordered as they prepared to go out onto Geonosis. "I'm not interested in getting into a war and maybe I can find a diplomatic solution to this mess."

"Don't worry. I've given up trying to argue with you," sighed Anakin, ordering R2 and C-3PO to guard the ship.

The pair made their way into the stalagmite city. As they passed through the columns they didn't notice that the surface of the pillars seemed to pulse with movement. High above, winged creatures detached themselves and hovered.

"Wait!" cried Anakin. But he sensed danger too late to prevent the attack. Three winged creatures swooped on him. He cut them down and pulled Padmé towards an exit. But this was merely a short walkway extending over a deep crevasse. Below it ran a conveyor belt. It seemed their only escape option. They jumped down and found themselves spirited into the centre of the droid factory. They ducked and wove across stamping machines and welders, all the time beating back the winged beings which swooped at them from above.

Anakin tripped on the assembly line and his right arm became locked in a molding device while Padmé got trapped in a vat about to be filled with molten metal.

Luckily R2-D2 had defied orders to stay with the ship and had come with C-3PO to their rescue. C-3PO dropped onto the conveyor belt to try to free Padmé but quickly found his head severed from his body. A droid head was screwed onto his body while a droid body was welded to his head.

"Oh! I'm so confused," he cried as the conveyor belt took him goodness knows where.

R2 however was more use. He managed to find the computer port controlling the vats and programmed Padmé's vat to dump her onto the walkway. Meanwhile Anakin manoeuvred his body away from the cutters and escaped the device but his lightsaber was cut in half.

"Not again!" he cried. "Obi-Wan's going to kill me."

Although they'd both escaped death in the foundry they now found themselves surrounded by the winged creatures and droidekas. Jango Fett dropped down from above, blaster in hand. "Don't move Jedi! Take them away," he ordered.

Dooku was taking no prisoners and within hours Anakin and Padmé found themselves tied to a cart parked in a gloomy tunnel. The tunnel opened out on to an enormous execution arena. From the noisy cheers a vast crowd had assembled to watch their end.

"Don't be afraid," Anakin told Padmé.

"I'm not afraid to die," she murmured. "I've been dying a little bit each day since you came back into my life."

Anakin was confused. "What are you saying?" he asked.

"I love you," she whispered.

Anakin wrenched himself around to face her. "You love me?! I thought we had decided not to fall in love. That we would be Forced to live a lie and it would destroy our lives..."

"I think our lives are about to be destroyed, anyway," she said, meeting his astonished gaze. "I truly, deeply love you, Anakin. Before we die I want you to know."

Padmé leaned towards Anakin and their lips met in a deep kiss.

But the moment was brief. With a crack of his whip the driver pushed the orray harnessed to the shafts of the cart into a gallop and the primitive vehicle jerked forward out of the tunnel and into the blinding sunlight of the arena.

The stadium was packed with tier upon tier of screaming Geonosians. The cart trundled to the centre. Padmé and Anakin were dismayed to see Obi-Wan already chained to one of four upright posts.

"I was beginning to wonder if you'd got my message," Obi-Wan called down to Anakin as he and Padmé were dragged from the cart and hoisted onto neighbouring posts.

"I retransmitted it as you requested Master," said Anakin. "Then we decided to come and rescue you."

"Good job!" muttered Obi-Wan sarcastically, as he watched the cart drive away leaving his friends chained up, arms pulled high above their heads.

"Let the executions begin." Came the call from Poggle the Lesser, Arch Duke of Geonosis. The crowd went wild. From three gates around the arena, great monsters were driven in. There was a bull-like reek, a lion-esque nexu and an acklay resembling a giant crustacean. Picadors carrying long spears rode in on orrays and prodded the snarling beasts towards the prisoners.

"I've got a bad feeling about this," said Anakin, watching the monsters toss their heads and roar.

"Relax, concentrate," ordered Obi-Wan.

"What about Padmé?" said Anakin.

Obi-Wan looked at the Senator. Using a wire she'd concealed within her robes, Padmé had successfully freed one of her hands from the handcuffs. She had pulled herself to the top of the post and was standing on it, trying to pull the chain from its binding.

"She seems to be on top of things," quipped Obi-Wan, impressed at her talent for escaping.

The fight was on. The acklay charged Obi-Wan but he ducked around the other side of the post leaving the acklay's claw to cut the chain of his restraints.

The nexu reared on its hind legs and attempted to swipe Padmé from the top of her pole. Its claws ripped through her shirt and drew blood, but she managed to whack it with the chain and it backed away. Anakin meanwhile, had wrapped his chains around the reek and leapt upon it, hoping its Force would break the chains. But it bucked him off and charged around the arena dragging Anakin in its wake. Finally freeing himself, he leapt again onto its back, whirled the free chain into the reek's mouth like a horse's bit and began to ride it.

"Jump!" He screamed at Padmé who had managed to work her chain loose but was again under assault from the nexu. Padmé leapt from her post onto the reek's back, holding tight to Anakin's robe and planting a kiss on his cheek. Now they just had to rescue Obi-Wan who was still fighting the acklay.

The Jedi threw a spear at full Force into the acklay's neck. This allowed him a moment in which to run away and leap up behind Anakin and Padmé.

"This isn't how it's supposed to be!" screamed Nute Gunray to Count Dooku in the archducal box. "Jango, finish her off!"

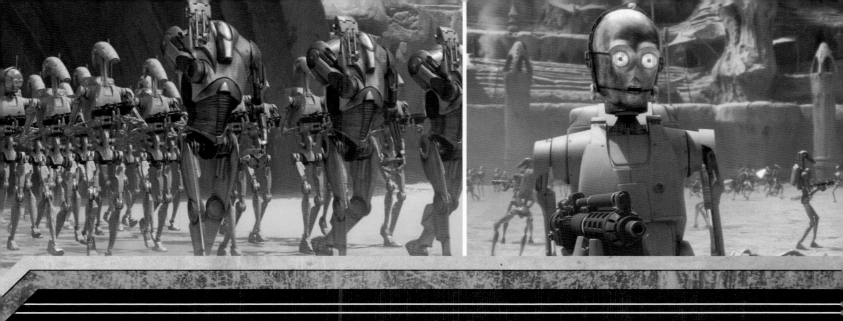

Dooku motioned for Jango to wait and smiled enigmatically at Nute. "Patience, Viceroy. She will die," he promised.

But, amid the uproar, no one had noticed an uninvited guest arrive in the box. Mace Windu ignited his lightsaber and held it to Jango Fett's Neck. Count Dooku turned, masking his surprise at this turn of events quite elegantly.

"Master Windu, how pleasant of you to join us," he smirked.

"This party's over," said Mace. Flashes of light burst around the arena as a hundred Jedi simultaneously switched on their lightsabers. The crowd fell silent. Count Dooku's lips curled in amusement.

"Brave," he said to Mace. "But foolish, my Jedi friend. You're impossibly outnumbered."

A legion of battle droids advanced down the corridor toward Mace firing their weapons. Mace deflected the blasts but Jango Fett fired his flamethrower at the Jedi, igniting his robe. Mace jumped into the arena where thousands more droids were pouring in. The battle began. Droids fired at the Jedi who deflected their bolts and felled them with their lightsabers. Mace and Ki-Adi-Mundi ran to the centre of the arena and re-armed Obi-Wan and Anakin. Ever resourceful, Padmé picked up a discarded pistol and joined the fight, blasting away at droids and Geonosians.

In the midst of the chaos the droid fixed to C-3PO's head entered the arena carrying a blaster rifle.

"What's all this noise? A battle! Oh no! I'm programmed for etiquette, not destruction," the polite robot stammered, surveying the scene of destruction.

Obi-Wan and Mace fought back to back, lightsabers flashing. Then the angry reek charged between an turned on Mace, who lost his lightsaber. Jango Fett saw his chance to finish the handicapped Jedi Master and leapt into the ring, but the reek almost trampled him and Mace, who'd retrieved his lightsaber with the Force and cut off Jango's head. From the safety of a tunnel, Boba watched his father's helmet roll across the ground.

The floor of the arena was now strewn with the bodies of Geonosians, droids and Jedi. But despite the Jedi's best efforts, and the slaying of all three monsters, the opposition was too strong. ReinForcements of super battle droids herded the remaining Jedi into the arena. On the encircling tiers above, thousands more battle droids levelled their weapons menacingly. In the archducal box Count Dooku lifted his hand and called out to the Jedi.

"Master Windu! You have fought gallantly. Worthy of recognition in the archives of the Jedi Order. Now it is finished," he paused. "Surrender and your lives will be spared."

"We will not be hostages to be bartered," cried Mace.

"Then I'm sorry, old friend," shouted the Count. At his signal every droid cocked its weapon. But suddenly…

"Look!" Padmé pointed skywards. Six gunships loomed into view. The Jedi could just make out the tiny figure of Yoda at the door of one of them.

"Around the survivors, a perimeter create" Yoda shouted.

The ships descended into the arena and landed in a cluster around the handful of Jedi. Clone troopers spilled out of every door and began firing up at the droids.

The surviving Jedi, including Ki-Adi-Mundi, Mace, Anakin, Obi-Wan and Padmé jumped onto two of the ships and hung on tight as they rose, still firing on the Separatists and droid army, out of the arena.

"If Dooku escapes, rally more systems to his cause, he will," Yoda told Mace as they surveyed the huge fleet of Trade Federation starships on Geonosis terrain.

"The Jedi have amassed a huge army," Nute Gunray told Count Dooku as they surveyed monitors and charts in their underground command centre. Every screen showed Republic gunships disgorging thousands of clone troopers which headed straight into combat with the Separatists' droids.

"How could the Jedi come up with an army so quickly?" asked a bemused Dooku.

"We must send all available droids into battle," screeched Nute.

"There are too many," said Dooku.

To make matters worse for the rebels, the Jedi had also managed to disable their communication meaning the Separatist's movements were further handicapped. On the ground clone troopers opened fire with artillery. Explosions wrecked many of the Geonosian's battle starships. Ranks of troopers advanced, firing at the massed droids. Others on speeder bikes engaged the Trade Federation's spider droids.

"This is not looking good at all," said Nute Gunray, watching as the ship containing Obi-Wan, Anakin and Padmé turned its fire on several of the Federation crafts.

"We must get the starships back into space," squeaked Rune Haako.

Count Dooku looked on in fury. "My Master will never allow the Republic to get away with this treachery," he roared.

"The Jedi must not find out designs for the ultimate weapon," said Poggle, ejecting a disc from the computerised display before him. "If they find out what we're planning to build, we're doomed."

"I'll take the designs with me to Coruscant," said Dooku, grabbing the disc. "They'll be much safer with my Master." The Count turned and ran into a hangar and taking off on a speeder bike. Two fighters flanked him as he jetted away.

"Concentrate all your fire on the nearest ship," Yoda told a clone commander as they watched the remaining Federation starships attempting to take off. Blast after blast rocked the nearest craft. It began to weaken under constant fire and finally exploded in a fireball.

Scanning the landscape from the open sides of the second Republic gunship, Anakin, Obi-Wan and Padmé caught sight of the fleeing Count.

"It's Dooku! Shoot him down!" said Anakin.

"We're out of rockets, sir," the clone captain replied.

There was no option but to follow him.

"We're going to need some help," warned Padmé.

"There isn't time!" said Obi-Wan. Anakin and I can handle this."

But Dooku wasn't ready to be captured. He signalled to the fighters flanking him. They veered off left and right, looped round and came up behind the Republic gunship. The clone captain put the gunship into a steep bank to avoid the fire and Padmé and two clone officers tumbled out of the open doorway.

"Put the ship down!" Anakin screamed to the pilot as he watched his love crash onto a sand dune below.

Obi-Wan grabbed his arm. "Don't let your personal feelings get in the way. I can't take Dooku alone. I need you," he implored. "If we catch him we can end this war right now. We have a job to do!"

"I don't care," Anakin yelled. He turned to the pilot. "Land the ship!"

"You will be expelled from the Jedi Order," Obi-Wan said. "Come to your senses. What do you think Padmé would do if she were in your position?"

Anakin's shoulders slumped. "She'd do her duty," he said resignedly as they flew away after Dooku.

At the command centre Yoda sensed Padmé was in trouble.

"The droid army is in full retreat," reported the clone commander.

"Well done, Commander," said Yoda. "Bring me a ship."

Meanwhile Count Dooku had reached a secret hangar contained in a stalagmite tower. He flew in and leapt from his speeder, running towards an interstellar solar sailer starship parked nearby. Anakin and Obi-Wan cut him off before he could reach it.

"You're going to pay for all the Jedi you killed today," Anakin told Dooku.

"We'll take him together," Obi-Wan whispered to Anakin. "You go in slowly on the left…"

But Anakin could not reign in his emotions. "No I'm taking him now!" he screamed, charging across the space at Dooku. Dooku just watched him come, then at the last moment thrust out an arm and unleashed a blast of Force lightning. Anakin was hurled across the room. He slammed into the opposite wall and slumped to the floor, semi-conscious.

"As you can see, my Jedi powers are far beyond yours," Dooku crowed. "Now back down." He unleashed another blast of Force lightning at Obi-Wan, but the Jedi blocked it easily with his lightsaber.

"I don't think so," he said.

Dooku smiled again and ignited his lightsaber in reply. Obi-Wan came in hard and fast, swinging at Count Dooku's head. But Dooku parried each blow with ease. A master of the old style Dooku was an elegant, graceful and deadly swordsman.

"Master Kenobi, you disappoint me. Yoda holds you in such high esteem," Dooku goaded as the pair locked lightsabers. Slowly but surely Dooku increased the tempo of his attack. His lightsaber swished menacingly, wounding Obi-Wan first in the arm, then the thigh. The brave Jedi stumbled then fell, his own weapon skittering across the floor. Grinning fiendishly, Dooku raised his weapon to finish Obi-Wan.

But he had underestimated Anakin. The Jedi-in-training was back on his feet and countered Dooku's near-fatal blow.

"Brave of you boy, but I'd have thought you had learned your lesson," sneered Dooku.

"I'm a slow learner," replied Anakin. Obi-Wan used the Force to catch his lightsaber and tossed it to Anakin. With two weapons, Anakin attacked. But despite his skill, there was no contest, Dooku parried and riposted every blow, disarming Anakin within seconds. Then in one flashing move he severed Anakin's arm at the elbow. Anakin flew across the hangar, landing unconscious by Obi-Wan's side. All seemed lost.

Then a diminutive but heroic figure entered the cave.

"Count Dooku," Yoda said politely.

"You have interfered with our affairs for the last time," Dooku yelled, using the Force to levitate machinery in the hangar and send it flying toward Yoda.

Extending his tiny arms, the Jedi Master stopped the flight of each foreign object, suspending it mid-air with incredible strength before sending it flying back towards Dooku.

"Powerful you have become, Dooku. The dark side I sense in you," Yoda said.

"I have become more powerful than any Jedi," laughed Dooku. "Even you."

"Much to learn you still have," said Yoda deflecting Force lightning thrown at him by the enraged Count.

"It is obvious this contest can not be decided by our knowledge of the Force, but by our skills with a lightsaber," said Dooku, whirling his weapon in a formal salute. Yoda barely had time to draw his weapon before Dooku charged. Their blades cross in a humming blur of light.

"Fought well, you have my old Padawan," said Yoda.

"This is just the beginning," screeched Dooku, using the Force to pull down one of the cranes in the hangar. It came crashing towards Obi-Wan and Anakin.

Yoda needed all his powers to prevent them being crushed to death and could only watch as Dooku ran up his ship's ramp and into the craft.

Just then Padmé arrived with two clone troopers. She had not been hurt by her fall and had ordered the troopers who had fallen with her to bring her to help the Jedi. They fired at Count Dooku, but were too late. The craft was already airborne and flew out of range before they could do much damage. Dooku had escaped. Seeing Anakin on the floor, Padmé ran to him and threw her arms around him. He was unconscious and mutilated, but at least he was alive.

Dooku's ship took him deep into the deserted old town of Coruscant. He manoeuvred into an empty building and touched down. Emerging, he walked across the room, towards a hooded figure who greeted him warmly.

"The Force is with us, Master Sidious," Dooku said.

"Welcome home, Lord Tyranus. You have done well," said Sidious.

"I have good news, my Lord. The war has begun," Dooku reported.

"Excellent," smiled Sidious. "Everything is going as planned.

In the Jedi Temple Obi-Wan and Mace Windu stood looking out at the great plaza below. Yoda sat in his chair.

"Do you believe what Dooku said about Sidious controlling the Senate?" Obi-Wan asked.

"Joined the dark side, Dooku has," said Yoda. "Lies, deceit, mistrust are his ways now."

"Nevertheless, I feel we should keep a closer eye

the Senate," said Mace, as Yoda nodded. "Where is our apprentice?" Mace asked.

"On his way to Naboo. Escorting Senator Amidala ome," Obi-Wan said.

e looked troubled. "I have to admit, that without the ones, it would not have been a victory."

"Victory, you say?" Yoda looked sad. "Not victory, aster Obi-Wan. The shroud of the dark side has llen. Begun, the Clone War has!"

From his balcony in the Senate Building, Chancellor Palpatine, Bail Organa, Mas Amedda and several other Senators looked down at the square. They watched sombrely as tens of thousands of clone troops moved forward in neat files to climb the ramps of the military assault ships lining the square. The sky above was already thick with transports. Yoda was right. The great Clone War had indeed begun.

But at a lake retreat on Naboo, in a beautiful garden, two young people had eyes only for each other. The Jedi apprentice and the Senator stood, hand-in-hand beneath a rose-covered arbour, overlooking the sparkling waters of the lake, while a holy man blessed their secret union. Witnessed only by C-3PO and R2-D2, Anakin Skywalker and Padmé Amidala sealed their secret union with a kiss.

COUNT DOOKU

Born on the planet Serenno to a noble and wealthy family, Dooku was taken as a small child to train as a Jedi. He became Qui-Gon Jinn's Master and spent over 70 years as a member of the Order. Well known for his skills with a lightsaber, Dooku settled disputes on many worlds. Yet his strong sense of independence and his challenging views—which he passed on to several of his Padawans—concerned many on the Jedi Council.

It comes as a blow to the Order when Dooku voluntarily renounces his Jedi commission after the Battle of Naboo. His belief that the Jedi weakened themselves by serving a corrupt Republic provokes him to disally himself from the Order. Dooku disappears for several years before emerging as a political firebrand, railing against corruption and fanning the flames of the Separatist movement.

The Jedi find it difficult to accept that Dooku is behind many of the worst aspects of the growing conflict between the Republic and the Separatists. What they don't know is that during his time away he was seduced by Darth Sidious to the power of dark side of the Force. Following Sith tradition, Dooku adopts the name Darth Tyranus. He then follows his Master's instructions and becomes a major force within the Separatist movement. Indeed, it is Dooku who chairs the meeting that formally creates the Confederacy of Independent Systems. He also finds others who will help destroy the Republic, such as Jango Fett, whom he recruits to be the template for a clone army. A very hands-on leader, he personally trains many of the greatest droid warriors in the Separatist army, including the Jedi-slaying General Grievous.

Dooku is ruthless, devious and has no problems conspiring against his former Jedi allies. However, he underestimates his Sith Master's ability to turn his back on him when a new, potentially more powerful apprentice emerges – Anakin Skywalker.

DID YOU KNOW?

The name Dooku is based on the Japanese word 'doku', meaning poison, but had to be changed to Dookan in Portuguese speaking countries, as there 'do cu' means 'from the bum'.

JANGO FETT

Born on Concord Dawn, Jango Fett grew up on a farm with his parents and sister. While he was still a boy, his family was murdered by the Death Watch, a chaotic splinter group of Mandalorian warriors who were hunting the true Mandalorian, Jaster Mereel. Jango helped Mereel escape and in return was taken in and protected by the warrior. Jaster trained Jango to become a fearsome fighter, with Fett proving his mettle during the Mandalorian Civil War. Once that conflict ended, he set himself up as a bounty hunter, soon getting a reputation as the best in the galaxy – as well as one of the most expensive.

Incredibly proficient in capturing or eliminating his prey, he wears a sleek suit based on Mandalorian battle armour. Fully equipped to defend himself from any adversary, Fett is armed with retractable wrist blades, dual pistols, a snare, and other concealed weaponry. His backpack is capable of jet propulsion and missile projection.

His exploits, including killing several Jedi, bring him to the attention of Count Dooku, who sees in Fett a great template for the clone army he's now in control of building. During a meeting that takes place around the moons of Bogden, Jango agrees to give up his DNA in return for a large payment and a single, unaltered clone, whom he dubs Boba. He wants the boy so that he can see all that he might have become if he had grown up with a loving and caring father.

Despite the money he makes being the template for the clones, Jango continues to work as a bounty hunter and is hired by the Trade Federation to assassinate Padmé Amidala. Fett tries to keep his identity secret during his missions, but his failure to kill Padmé leads Obi-Wan Kenobi to follow him to Kamino, where the Jedi discovers both Jango and the almost complete droid army.

DID YOU KNOW?

Jango Fett helped with the design of the clone trooper uniform, as evidenced by the similar shape of his Mandalorian helmet and the ones worn by the first clones.

CLONE TROOPER

All clone troopers share Jango Fett's basic DNA, but they have been genetically altered to ensure that they are particularly skilled in combat and unwaveringly loyal to the Galactic Republic and the Supreme Chancellor in particular. Their growth and mental structures are accelerated so that they reach maturity in only half the time it would take a normal person. As clones, they are virtually indistinguishable from one another in physical appearance, mental acuity and stamina. Their training regimens differ though, creating numerous classes of troopers from pilots to commandos.

The clones are built on Kamino in Tipoca City. The Kaminoan cloners believe they're working on the orders of the Jedi (and therefore on behalf of the Senate), but the army is actually part of a secret plan by the Sith to start a Galactic Civil War. The Kaminoans are dedicated to perfecting the production of the army, giving each trooper the exact amount of training and socialisation needed to create sound soldiers. It's not an infallible process though, as around seven in every 200 clones needs to be reconditioned in order to normalise them.

When war breaks out, the Republic makes use of this ready-made army. Most, including the Jedi, come to trust the unswerving loyalty of the troopers, who (with the exception of a few aberrations) are unable to disobey orders and are ready to die in defence of the Republic. This trust comes back to haunt the Jedi when Palpatine issues the infamous Order 66, which directs the clones to kill all Jedi. After the Clone Wars, the clones are redesignated as stormtroopers and become ruthless enforcers of the Empire.

DID YOU KNOW?

Every clone trooper stands 1.78 metres tall without a helmet.

BATTLE DROID

Clone Troopers stand on one side of the Clone Wars and battle droids on the other. There have been many droids built for fighting over the centuries, but by far the largest droid army ever assembled is the one the Trade Federation creates during the last years of the Galactic Republic. The battle droid army is built upon and expanded in the years running up to the Clone Wars as the Separatist movement edges ever closer to all-out battle.

There are many types of battle droids that are skilled in different things, from being infantry footsoldiers to pilots. Droids have many benefits over humans and some drawbacks too. For example, it takes clone troopers ten years to mature but droids can be built quickly and used to flood the battlefield. Indeed this becomes one of the major points of contention after the Trade Federation uses battle droids to invade Naboo, as the sheer number of droids allows the Trade Federation to take control of the planet in a matter of hours. Subsequent treaties are put in place to limit the production of new droids, but the Trade Federation and Separatist movement continue to keep the foundries running at full capacity.

Many battle droids are not programmed for independent thinking, with their intelligence derived from a central source aboard a control ship. Their almost perfect discipline makes them easier to manage than a human army but can also be a major drawback, as their ultimate defeat at Naboo proves. When Anakin Skywalker destroys the droid control ship, the entire droid army is rendered useless and the Trade Federation is forced to retreat. The Separatists quickly learn from this and create a far more diverse and less dependent army of droids, which prove a fearsome enemy during the Clone Wars.

DID YOU KNOW?

The main type of droid seen during the Battle of Naboo is the B1 battle droid, mainly designed to defeat the enemy through sheer numbers.

STAR WARS™
EPISODE III
REVENGE OF THE SITH™

The Republic is crumbling under attacks by the ruthless Sith Lord, Count Dooku. There are heroes on both sides. Evil is everywhere.

In a stunning move, the fiendish droid leader, General Grievous, has swept into the Republic capital and kidnapped Chancellor Palpatine, leader of the Galactic Senate.

As the Separatist droid army attempts to flee the besieged capital with their valuable hostage, two Jedi Knights lead a desperate mission to rescue the captive Chancellor....

CHEWBACCA

Born on the tree-covered planet of Kashyyyk, from his youth Chewbacca was known for his sense of adventure. Unlike most other Wookiees, he spent much of his time away from his homeworld. During his travels he became highly conversant in mechanics and the workings of starships.

He is renowned for his loyalty, which has often been tested at great personal risk to the fur-covered Wookiee. No matter what the situation, he is the conscience of those around him, with his strong moral compass rarely steering him wrong. These aren't the only qualities that have made him a great friend and companion in the 200 years that he's been alive, as when the situation calls for it, he becomes a fearsome fighter. His great size (he's over two metres tall) and strength allow him to rip many creatures limb from limb. His favoured weapon is the bowcaster, a hand-crafted crossbow-like device that shoots bolts of energy. He also often has a bandolier slung over his left shoulder that contains plenty of extra firepower.

He rises to prominence during the Clone Wars, becoming one of the leading members of the Wookiee resistance to the Separatists. During the Battle of Kashyyyk, he is part of the Republic High Command alongside fellow Wookiee Tarfful and Jedi Master Yoda. After the start of the Jedi Purge, the ever-loyal Chewbacca helps Yoda escape the planet and go into exile. When the Clone Wars end, Chewbacca fights against the Empire and is eventually put into a forced labour camp. He is saved from almost certain death at the camp by a man called Han Solo, and becomes the first mate on Solo's starship.

DID YOU KNOW?

Chewbacca is married to Mallatobuck and has a son called Lumpawarrump (or Lumpy for short).

MACE WINDU

Alongside Yoda and Count Dooku, Mace Windu is considered one of the greatest masters of the lightsaber in the galaxy. His battle skills are so distinguished that he even invented a new fighting style, known as Vaapad. He is willing to sacrifice himself for any cause he believes is worthy and has faced death numerous times while he tries to keep peace in the galaxy. It's not just his abilities with a lightsaber that are legendary, but also his profound wisdom and great accomplishments. Even though he's only 40-years-old at the time of the Invasion of Naboo, his command of the Force is considered second only Yoda's.

From the outside, many see Mace as a sombre figure who leads by rigorous example, using concrete guidelines and steady discipline to achieve his aims. This belies the fact that he is often the first to laugh at a joke and enjoys springing deep philosophical traps during debates, in order to provoke thought both in himself and others. He is not quick to trust when he senses potential conflict, and as a result he is wary of the angry and fearful Anakin Skywalker. Of all those on the Jedi High Council, it is Mace who is most vocal in his uncertainty over Anakin, especially when Skywalker begins to get close to Chancellor Palpatine.

As both a fighter and member of the Jedi High Council, he becomes a vital force during the Clone Wars. His skill as a warrior results in him leading one of the first major skirmishes of the war, taking a Jedi strike force to Geonosis to take on Count Dooku and rescue Anakin Skywalker, Obi-Wan Kenobi and Padmé Amidala. Several years later the great warrior nearly brings the war – and the fledgling Empire – to an end when he takes on Darth Sidious in battle, but he doesn't reckon on just how conflicted Anakin Skywalker is. Striking down Windu in the service of Sidious completes Anakin's journey to the dark side.

DID YOU KNOW?

Mace Windu is the only Jedi in the films to carry a purple-bladed lightsaber (apparently at the request of actor Samuel L. Jackson).

SENATOR BAIL ORGANA

A member of the royal family of Alderaan, from his youth Bail has been trained to be Viceroy and First Chairman of the Alderaan system, and a member of the Galactic Senate. His ascension was not without incident though as shortly before he became Viceroy, a dispute broke out over the appropriate lineage for the title. It was only sorted out after a Jedi envoy negotiated a settlement. As a result, Bail became a staunch ally of the Jedi Order for the rest of his life.

Although he's known to be somewhat cynical, he's nevertheless one of the greatest believers in the Republic and the democracy he thinks it should represent. He is part of a trusted inner circle close to Chancellor Palpatine, unaware that the head of the Senate is really Sith Lord Darth Sidious. An impassioned supporter of civic virtue, Bail regrets that to counter the Separatist threat, the Republic must deploy the newly discovered clone army. He cannot deny though that part of him is glad that after years of bureaucracy and stalemating, at least some action is being taken against the Separatists.

Initially he stands by in reluctant support of the Clone Wars, but when he is informed by former Chancellor Valorum that information about the conflict is being withheld from the Senate, he begins to question the war. After he witnesses the destruction of the ship carrying Valorum, he is certain there is something amiss in the Senate and becomes resolute in challenging the increasing war powers being granted to Palpatine.

Bail is determined not to allow democracy to disappear without a fight. When Palpatine springs his trap to try and destroy the Jedi, Bail is there to help. In the hope that one day the new Empire will be defeated, Bail agrees to raise the orphaned child Leia, the daughter of Padmé Amidala and the fallen Jedi Anakin Skywalker.

DID YOU KNOW?

In Episode I, Adrian Dunbar was going to play Bail Organa, but his scenes were eventually cut, with Jimmy Smits taking on the role in Episodes II & III.

OWEN LARS

Owen, the son of Cliegg Lars, was born on the core world of Ator. He went to his father's homeworld, Tatooine, after his mother died when he was just a boy. Not a particularly adventurous person, Owen prefers pragmatic and achievable goals. He has worked hard since childhood to make a life for himself, and he is determined to ensure the moisture farm he and his father run is the most productive it can be. Apart from work, his only other objective is the pursuit of his beloved, Beru Whitesun.

He helps Cliegg purchase the slave Shmi Skywalker, along with the protocol droid C-3PO, and supports his dad when he frees Shmi and the two marry. Owen soon comes to think of Shmi as his mother and is saddened by the fact that Anakin's absence in her life continues to cause her pain. Tragedy strikes when Shmi is kidnapped by Tusken Raiders in an attack that also results in Cliegg losing a leg. A month afterwards, Owen meets Anakin for the first time, when the Jedi turns up hoping to rescue Shmi. Owen is not surprised to see him, as he has long sensed that someday Anakin would come seeking his mother. Unfortunately the Jedi is too late and returns Shmi's body to the moisture farm.

Owen's most important role begins after the Clone Wars, when Obi-Wan Kenobi arrives on Tatooine with Owen's nephew, Luke. Obi-Wan convinces Owen and Beru to look after the child, keeping the baby far from the eyes of the Empire. Lars is determined to raise Luke as a normal child, in the hope that he can prevent him from suffering the same fate as his father, Anakin.

DID YOU KNOW?

In the prequel trilogy, Owen Lars was played by a young, unknown Joel Edgerton, who's since gone on to become the star of movies such as *Warrior* and *The Thing*.

War! The Republic was crumbling under attacks...

The Separatists led by the ruthless Sith Count Dooku. Evil was everywhere. The fiendish droid leader General Grievous had kidnapped Chancellor Palpatine, leader of the Galactic Senate.

As the Separatist droid army attempted to flee Coruscant with their valuable hostage, two Jedi Knightsled a desperate mission to rescue the captive Chancellor.

"Master, General Grievous' ship is directly ahead – the one crawling with vulture droids," Anakin radioed to Obi-Wan. The pair, accompanied by their trusty droids R2-D2 and R4-P17, were piloting separate starfighters into battle above the city of Coruscant.

"I see it," Obi-Wan replied, clocking the enormous Trade Federation cruiser up ahead. The hull was crawling with bat-like vulture droids. "Odd Ball, do you copy?" he radioed. "Mark my position. Form your squad up behind me."

"We're on your tail, General Kenobi," came the reply.

Four droid tri-fighters joined the vulture droids heading for the Republic ships.

"This is where the fun begins," smiled Anakin, always in his element in the air.

Obi-Wan and Anakin split up, letting the tri-fighters pass between them, then closed in behind, blasting them out of the sky.

Seeing several of their clone fighters hit, Anakin decided to break formation.

"I'm going to help them out!" he yelled.

"No!" cried Obi-Wan. "They're doing their job so we can do ours."

With a nifty barrel roll spin Anakin avoided several droid missiles, which collided and exploded behind him.

Obi-Wan was not so lucky. A clutch of buzz droids

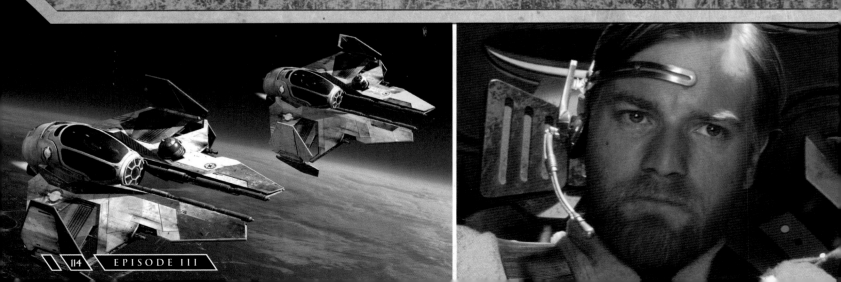

landed on his ship and began to tear it apart. One even ripped off R4's head and tossed it away.

"Oh dear," exclaimed Obi-Wan, watching the disc of metal spin off into space.

"The buzz droids are shutting down my controls," Obi-Wan shouted.

"Move to the right, so I can get a clear shot at them," said Anakin.

He pulled his fighter alongside Obi-Wan's ship and vaporized the buzz droids on the left wing, unfortunately he also destroyed the wing.

"Hold your fire! You're not helping here," Obi-Wan cried.

Anakin backed off, but the buzz droids continued to dismantle Obi-Wan's ship.

Next, Anakin tried knocking them off by crashing into Obi-Wan, but five clung on and Obi-Wan's ship was badly dented in the process.

"Hold on Anakin. You're going to get us both killed! Get out of here. There's nothing more you can do," said Obi-Wan.

But Anakin refused to leave his Master. Another bump knocked all the buzz droids off Obi-Wan's ship.

However, the last one crawled on to Anakin's wing and began attacking R2-D2. R2 whirled round, extended an arm and hit the buzz droid with a stream of electricity that knocked it into space.

The Jedi starfighters flew in unison towards the General's command ship but Obi-Wan's craft was disintegrating further by the second.

"I have a bad feeling about this," said Obi-Wan, as they flew shield door into the main hanger and screeched onto the deck in a fantail of sparks.Obi-Wan was just able to cut himself free from his cockpit before his entire ship exploded.

Buzz droids rushed at him from all directions as Anakin leapt from his starfighter and joined his friend. The Jedi Knights' lightsabers hummed as they cut through the droids.

When the last of the droids was destroyed, Obi-Wan and Anakin joined R2 at a computer wall socket. R2 beeped as he beamed out a hologram of the ship for the Jedi to see.

"The Chancellor's signal is coming from the observation platform at the top of that spire," said Obi-Wan.

"I sense Count Dooku" said Anakin.

"I sense a trap," Obi-Wan added.

The pair's next move was to spring the trap. Obi-Wan tossed a communications link to R2 and Anakin told the droid to stay with the ship.

General Grievous was already aware of their presence. As the Jedi waited for an elevator to take them to the observation platform, they turned to see three destroyer droids approaching.

They deflected their bolts and backed into the elevator which arrived just in time. The doors closed and Obi-Wan sighed in relief until…

"Drop your weapons!" Came the order. The lift was full of battle droids. With lightning reflexes, the Jedi activated their lightsabers and destroyed them all.

But more trouble was in store. The lift shuddered to a halt between floors. Obi-Wan contacted R2 and asked him to re-activate the lift but R2 was in hiding from several super battle droids who had discovered the Jedi starfighters in the hangar.

Anakin cut a hole in the ceiling of the lift and jumped through. Just at that point the droids left the hangar and R2 re-activated the lift.

Anakin just had time to grab onto the entry door before the lift plunged down the shaft and disappeared.

"Whoa, R2," shouted Obi-Wan, "we need to be going up."

R2 sent the lift upwards just as two battle droids prised open the doors where Anakin was hanging. They cocked their weapons but he jumped onto the lift roof as it passed by.

"Oh, it's you…" said Obi-Wan as Anakin dropped back into the lift through the hole. When the elevator finally arrived at the floor containing the observation platform, the Jedi carefully made their way to the General's quarters.

At one end sat Chancellor Palpatine, restraints holding him in a chair. He looked utterly distressed.

"Are you alright?" Anakin asked.

"Count Dooku," said the Chancellor, staring past them towards the door.

Obi-Wan and Anakin looked round to see Dooku stride into the room.

"This time we'll do it together," Obi-Wan whispered, referring to their last encounter with Dooku, when Anakin's haste had led to the loss of his arm.

"Get help!" cried Palpatine. "You're no match for him. He's a Sith Lord."

Obi-Wan smiled reassuringly at the Chancellor. "Chancellor Palpatine, Sith Lords are our speciality," he said.

With that, the pair charged Dooku and a great lightsaber battle began.

"My powers have doubled since the last time we met, Count," boasted Anakin.

"Good," smirked Dooku. "Twice the pride, double the fall."

The fight was intense and Dooku seemed to have the upper hand. He kicked Anakin across the room then grabbed Obi-Wan in a choke-hold, sending his unconscious body to the floor and using the Force to cause a section of the balcony to crash down onto the Jedi.

Anakin came round and leapt at Dooku before he could kill Obi-Wan.

"I sense great fear in you, Skywalker. You have hate, you have anger, but you don't use them," Dooku goaded, as the young Jedi span at him with a flying kick.

This comment made Anakin attack the Count with a new ferociousness and in one, final, energized charge he cut off the Count's hands, catching his lightsaber as it fell.

Dooku fell to his knees as Anakin placed the two lightsabers at his neck.

A chilling voice piped up from the other side of the room.

"Good Anakin, good. Kill him. Kill him now," breathed Palpatine.

Dooku looked fearfully at Palpatine, then up at Anakin who was shaking his head.

"Do it!!" yelled Palpatine and in one stroke Anakin severed Dooku's head. Afterwards the young Jedi apprentice hung his head in shame. "He was an unarmed prisoner. I shouldn't have done that. It's not the Jedi way," he said, releasing Palpatine.

The Chancellor rubbed his wrists. "It's only natural," he said. "He cut off your arm, you wanted revenge."

But Anakin wasn't listening; he rushed to Obi-Wan and lifted the masonry from his legs, pulling him free. Palpatine tried to get him to leave his mentor but he would not.

"His fate will be the same as ours," he said, hoisting Obi-Wan onto his shoulders.

The ship came under fire from clone troopers and the heroes were thrown down the lift shaft.

As they hung there, using the strength of Anakin's robotic arm, Obi-Wan regained consciousness.

"Did I miss something?" he asked, glancing down at a bottomless pit.

The Jedi managed to throw out grappling hooks and swung themselves and Palpatine through an open door into a hallway before the re-started elevator roared by. But before they could make their escape from the hangar, they were captured by super battle droids.

"General Grievous. You're shorter than I expected," joked Anakin as they stood before the monstrous droid on the bridge of his ship.

"Jedi scum," coughed Grievous, sweeping his cloak behind him. "Your lightsabers will make a fine addition to my collection." He slipped the Jedi's confiscated sabers into his cloak lining.

"Not this time," cried Obi-Wan. He called to R2 who created a diversion by shooting out electrical pulses. Then Obi-Wan used the Force to yank their lightsabers from the general's cloak.

Deftly, he cut the bonds around his and Anakin's hands.

"Crush them. Make them suffer," rasped Grievous, pushing his battle droids into combat with the Jedi.

But Anakin and Obi-Wan were too powerful and within seconds had overcome the droids.

With one mighty blow, Grievous struck his electrified staff into the window. It smashed and everything which wasn't nailed down was sucked out into space – including himself!

Obi-Wan, Anakin and Palpatine held on for dear life until a blast shield closed around the space where the window used to be and they were able to find their feet.

Meanwhile, Grievous was not spinning through space. He had fired a cable from his arm, attached it to the ship and swung back onto the hull.

He crawled along using his magnetic hands and fee to an airlock, entered the ship, jumped into an escape pod and blasted off.

On their way from the bridge to the hangar Anakin and Obi-Wan continued to cut through droids as if they were butter. Palpatine watched in shock and awe, flinching at each shower of sparks.

"Grievous!" gasped Obi-Wan, noticing all the escape pods had been launched. He turned to Anakin and indicated a broken-up Trade Federation cruiser.

"Can you fly a cruiser like this?" he asked Anakin.

"Under the circumstances I'd say the ability to pilot what's left of this thing is irrelevant," replied Anakin, manically flicking switches. As he took off, a large part of the ship broke away and got left behind. The nose and cockpit, containing the heroes burned up like a fireball as they flew, leaving a trail of debris in its wake.

"We're coming in too hot," yelled Anakin as they streaked across the Coruscant skyline.

Palpatine and Obi-Wan clung on as the ship rattled towards an industrial landing platform. Even R2 made a noise which sounded like a scream.

"Another happy landing," sighed Obi-Wan, as the smoking ship crash landed under safety foam jets of five Republic fireships.

Later, Anakin and Obi-Wan took their leave of each other in the Senate Building.

"Are you coming, Master?" asked Anakin.

"I'm not brave enough for politics. I have to report to the Council. Besides, someone needs to be the poster boy. You rescued me from the buzz droids, killed Count Dooku and rescued the Chancellor!"

"All because of your training," replied Anakin.

"Let's be fair," said Obi-Wan. "Today, you are the hero and you deserve your glorious day with the politicians."

The Chancellor approached Mace Windu.

"Are you alright?" Mace asked.

"Yes, thanks to your Jedi Knights," replied Palpatine. "They killed Dooku but Grievous has escaped again," he continued. "He is leader of the droid army and the Senate will vote to continue the war as long as Grievous is alive."

Mace assured Palpatine the Council would make finding Grievous their highest priority.

After receiving thanks from Senator Bail Organa, Anakin ran towards a familiar shadow lurking near a pillar.

"Oh Anakin!" sighed Padmé, embracing the Jedi with relief. "There were whispers you'd been killed."

"I'm alright," said Anakin. "It feels we've been apart for a lifetime," he bent to kiss Padmé again.

"Not here," she said, stepping back.

"Yes, here!" said Anakin, "I'm tired of all this deception. I don't care if they know we're married." He broke off, noticing how she trembled in his arms.

"What's going on?" he asked. He could never have anticipated the reply. Padmé was pregnant.

"This is the happiest moment of my life," he smiled, kissing her deeply.

General Grievous landed on the planet Utapau. He made his way to the conference room where he received a hologram from Darth Sidious.

"General Grievous," said Sidious, "I suggest you move the Separatist leaders to Mustafar. The end of the war is near."

"But the loss of Count Dooku…" said the General.

"His death was necessary," rasped Sidious. "Soon I will have a new apprentice, one far younger and more powerful."

Padmé stood on the balcony of her apartment brushing her hair as Anakin looked on lovingly.

They talked excitedly about their plans for the future. Padmé suggested returning to the Lake Country on Naboo to where they could have the baby in private.

But that night, a new nightmare plagued Anakin. He saw Padmé on a table in an alien medical chamber. She screamed for his help before dying.

Anakin awoke in a panic. He was drenched with sweat. He got up leaving the sleeping Padmé and went onto the veranda. A while later Padmé awoke and went looking for him.

"What's bothering you?" she asked.

"I remember when I gave this to you," he told her, touching the snippet of Japor he'd given her as a boy.

She wore it round her neck.

"How long is it going to take for us to be honest with each other?" she asked.

Anakin revealed his dream – so similar to those about his mother – which had plagued him before her kidnap and murder at the hands of Tusken Raiders on Tatooine.

"You die in childbirth," he told her.

"It was only a dream," she said trying to sooth Anakin.

"I won't let this one become real," he added with determination.

Next morning, Anakin sought out Yoda and told him he'd dreamt of death.

"Someone you know?" enquired the Jedi Master. Anakin nodded.

"Someone close to you?" asked Yoda. Again Anakin nodded.

Yoda told him he must be careful for the fear of loss is a path to the dark side. When Anakin said he would not let his vision come to pass, Yoda told him that death is a natural part of life.

"Rejoice for those who transform into the Force," Yoda said. "Mourn them, do not. Attachment leads to jealousy."

"What must I do, Master Yoda?" asked the anxious Jedi.

"Train yourself to let go of everything you fear to lose," said Yoda.

Anakin rushed straight off to the briefing room but missed the report on the Outer Rim sieges. He apologised to Obi-Wan who had waited for him.

Obi-Wan told him the sieges were going well but that the Senate was expected to vote more executive powers to Chancellor Palpatine.

"Well that can only mean less deliberating and more action. It will make it easier for us to end this war," said Anakin.

"Be careful of your friend Palpatine," Obi-Wan warned.

Anakin frowned. "Careful of what?"

Obi-Wan told him that Palpatine had requested Anakin's presence but had not informed the Council.

"It is unusual and it's making me uneasy," said Obi-Wan.

When Anakin arrived at the Senator's office, Palpatine had an unexpected and irregular request.

"I'm depending on you to be the eyes, ears and voice of the Republic and I'm appointing you to be my personal representative on the Jedi Council," he told the delighted Anakin.

"But the Council elects its own members. They'll never accept this," said Anakin.

"I think they will," replied Palpatine. "They need you, more than you know."

The Council accepted the young Jedi, but only begrudgingly.

"Allow this appointment lightly, the Council does not," said Yoda. Anakin nodded reverently.

"You are on this Council," explained Mace, "but we do not grant you the rank of Master."

Anakin's temper flared. "What? This is outrageous, unfair. How can you be on the Council and not be a Master?" he yelled. He took his place, trying hard to regain his composure.

The session heard updates from various Jedi Knights, some appeared via hologram as they were in battle.

Ki-Adi-Mundi was ordered to sweep the outlying systems of the Outer Rim for General Grievous, while Yoda agreed to take a battalion of clones to reinforce the Wookiees who were being invaded on Kashyyyk.

Anakin listened, disappointment clouding his features. He'd been excluded from all the action.

That evening he confided in his mentor.
"Put me on the Council and not make me a Master? It's insulting!" he fumed.

Obi-Wan told him to be calm, saying he should be honoured to be the youngest person ever admitted to the Council. He said the denial of rank was due to his closeness to Palpatine.

"The Council doesn't like it when he interferes in Jedi affairs," said Obi-Wan.

"I didn't ask to be put on the Council," huffed Anakin.

"No, but it's what you wanted," replied Obi-Wan. He took a deep breath before his next revelation.

"The Council wants you to report on the Chancellor's dealings," he said.

"Spy on the Chancellor?" Anakin was incensed. "That's treason."

Obi-Wan said the assignment was to be secret. "Our allegiance is to the Senate, not to its leader who has managed to stay in office long after his term has expired. Something is out of place."

"You're asking me to do something against the Jedi Code. Against the Republic. Against a friend. That's what's out of place," fumed Anakin.

Obi-Wan conveyed Anakin's worries about the mission as he and Mace escorted Yoda to the gunship that would transport him to Kashyyyk.

"It's dangerous putting Anakin and Palpatine together," said Mace. "I don't think the boy can handle it. I don't trust him."

"Is he not the Chosen One?" said Obi-Wan "Is he not to destroy the Sith and bring balance to the Force?"

"The prophecy, misread, could have been," reflected Yoda.

Obi-Wan stood up for his apprentice. "He will not let me down. He never has," he stated loyally.

"I hope that right, you are," Yoda replied, heading towards the gunship.

As the sun set over Coruscant, Anakin and Padmé talked on their balcony.

"I sometimes wonder what's happening to the Jedi Order," said Anakin. "This war is destroying the principles of the Republic."

"Have you ever considered we may be on the wrong side?" asked Padmé. "What if the democracy we thought we were serving no longer exists, and the Republic has become the very evil we've been fighting to destroy?"

"You're sounding like a Separatist,"said Anakin, getting up from the sofa in annoyance.

"This war represents a failure to listen." Padmé continued. "You're close to the Chancellor. Please ask him to stop the fighting and let diplomacy resume."

The request angered Anakin. "Make a motion to the Senate, where that kind of request belongs," he snapped.

Padmé apologised and went to him. Anakin held her, losing himself in her embrace.

A few nights later the Chancellor again requested Anakin's presence. Anakin found him in his box at the Galaxies Opera House.

"Our clone intelligence units have discovered the location of General Grievous. He is hiding in the Utapau system," revealed Palpatine.

"At last we'll be able to capture him and end this war," said Anakin as Palpatine dismissed his aides.

"Anakin, you know I'm not able to rely on the Jedi Council," Palpatine continued. "You must sense what I have come to suspect – that the Council want control of the Republic and are planning to betray me."

Anakin looked unsure. "I know they don't trust you," he said.

"Or the Senate, the Republic or even democracy for that matter," hissed Palpatine.

Anakin admitted his trust in the Jedi Council had been shaken. He said nothing of his secret assignment.

"They asked you to spy on me, didn't they?" asked Palpatine. "All who gain power are afraid to lose it – even the Jedi."

"The Jedi use their power for good," argued Anakin.

"The Sith and Jedi are similar in almost every way, including their quest for greater power," said Palpatine.

Anakin shook his head. "The Sith think inward only about themselves. The Jedi are selfless and only care about others."

Palpatine told Anakin the story of Darth Plagueis. According to legend, Plagueis was a Sith Lord so powerful he could use the dark side of the Force to influence the midi-chlorians so he could save people from death.

"Is it possible to learn this power?" Anakin asked.

"Not from a Jedi," said Palpatine.

At the next Council meeting, Anakin relayed the Chancellor's thoughts on General Grievous' whereabouts.

"A partial message was intercepted from Utapau," he told Yoda, who appeared by hologram from Kashyyyk.

"Act on this, we must," Yoda ordered.

"The Chancellor has requested I lead the campaign," said Anakin confidently. Every Council member looked at him, disturbed.

"A Master is needed, with more experience," said Yoda. Ki-Adi-Mundi promptly suggested Obi-Wan Kenobi and all the Jedi concurred. Anakin was, once again, disappointed.

Yoda had other things to think about than the frustrations of his youngest Council member. It was time to lead the clone troops and Wookiees into battle against the Separatist droid army. A Wookiee chieftain let out an ear shattering roar and rushed off the beach into the water where the first of many spider droids was emerging from the watery depths.

Back on Coruscant, Anakin walked Obi-Wan to the landing platform. They watched the thousands of clone troops and weaponry being loaded onto a massive Republic assault ship. As Obi-Wan turned to leave Anakin called him back.

"I've disappointed you," he said sadly. "I haven't been very appreciative. I've been arrogant and I apologise, I've just been so frustrated with the Council," said Anakin.

"You are strong and wise Anakin," smiled Obi-Wan, placing a paternal arm round his apprentice's shoulders. "I'm proud of you. I have trained you since you were a boy. I have taught you everything I know and you have become a far greater Jedi than I could hope to be. Be patient, Anakin. It will not be long before the Council makes you a Jedi Master."

"May the Force be with you," said Anakin softly.

"Goodbye, old friend," replied Obi-Wan. "May the Force be with you."

He headed down the ramp towards the waiting Republic battle cruiser and headed off on his mission.

In the hangar of the battle cruiser Obi-Wan and clone commander Cody discussed tactics over a hologram of the planet Utapau, projected by R4.

"I'll keep them distracted until you get there," Obi-Wan told Cody. "Just don't take too long."

"Come on, when have I ever let you down?" replied Cody.

"Very well," laughed Obi-Wan. "The burden is on me not to destroy all the droids until you arrive."

Still chuckling to himself, he climbed into his Jedi starfighter, whizzed out of the cruiser and hyperjumped for Utapau.

Left with too much time on his hands and still plagued by his worrying dream about Padmé's death, Anakin had become jealous.

"Obi-Wan's been here, hasn't he?" he asked Padmé, sensing his Master's presence in the room. Padmé told him that Obi-Wan had visited that morning.

"What did he want?" Anakin asked.

"He's worried about you. Says you've been under a lot of stress." Padmé walked into the bedroom. Anakin followed.

"I feel lost," he admitted. "Obi-Wan and the Council don't trust me. I'm not the Jedi I should be. I want more, and I know I shouldn't."

They stopped in front of the window and Anakin put his hands on Padmé's belly. "I've found a way to save you," he told her. She looked confused.

"...from my nightmares," he added. "Is that what's bothering you?" she asked.

"I won't lose you, Padmé," he said. "I'm not going to die in childbirth Ani. I promise you," she said.

Padmé sought to understand the shift in Anakin's attitude while he tried to remind himself that the decision he was about to take, was the right one.

Obi-Wan landed his ship on Utapau and was met by Tion Medon, a local administrator.

"Greetings, young Jedi," said Tion. "What brings you to our remote sanctuary?"

"Unfortunately, the war," replied Obi-Wan.

"There is no war here unless you've brought it with you," said Tion.

Obi-Wan shook his head and told the alien he simply wanted fuel and to use the city as a base to search nearby star systems for General Grievous.

As Tion gestured to ground crew to refuel Obi-Wan's fighter he leaned forward and whispered that Grievous was already in the city, on the 10th level, with thousands of battle droids, and that the locals were all hostages.

"Tell your people to take shelter," said Obi-Wan. "If you have warriors, now is the time."

He climbed back into his fighter as if to take off. Watching Grievous' bodyguards retreat from the overhead platform, he told R4 to fly the fighter back to the ship and tell Cody he'd found Grievous. Then, checking the landing platform was clear; he climbed back down to watch his fighter fly off.

A movement on the wall of the sheer cliff behind him alerted Obi-Wan to the presence of a huge lizard. He called it to him, mounted and made his way up the wall to the tenth level.

There, as Tion Medon had said, General Grievous was addressing the Separatist council. Nute Gunray, Rune Haako, Poggle the Lesser and Shu Mai were among the many gathered.

"The armies of the Republic will track us here," rasped Grievous. "I'm sending you to the Mustafar system in the Outer Rim. It's a volcanic planet. You'll be safe there."

"Palpatine managed to escape your grip, General," scoffed Nute. "Without Dooku, I have doubts about your ability to keep us safe."

Grievous shot him a murderous look.

"Be thankful, Viceroy, you have not found yourself in my grip. Go. Your ship is waiting."

When the room emptied, Obi-Wan removed his cloak and jumped down off his lizard behind Grievous.

"Hello, there!" he said, cheerily.

"General Kenobi," said Grievous, "you are a bold one." He turned to his droid bodyguards. "Kill him!"

But Obi-Wan used the Force to bring a chunk of ceiling down on the guards, smashing them to pieces. Reinforcement battle droids surged forwards, surrounding the Jedi.

"Back away, I will deal with this Jedi slime myself," coughed Grievous.

He sneered at Obi-Wan.

"You fool. I have been trained in your Jedi arts by Count Dooku," he said. With that his arms separated and he grabbed four lightsabers from his cloak. His limbs whirred in a flashing display of swordsmanship.

Obi-Wan was hard pressed to defend himself against the onslaught.

Just as they locked blades a loud explosion echoed through the sinkhole outside.

The generals glanced out to see clone troops advancing on the battle droids outside.

"Army or not, you must realise you are doomed," snarled Grievous.

"Oh, I don't think so," said Obi-Wan using the Force to hurl Grievous backwards up into the ceiling.

He fell onto a lower platform and Obi-Wan jumped down after him, but Grievous was already up and away, racing spider-like on all his limbs towards one of the landing platforms.

With lasers and bullets ripping through the air around him the General jumped onto a wheel bike and took off down the ramp, almost slicing Obi-Wan as he passed.

Obi-Wan whistled loudly for his lizard, jumped on its back and sped off in hot pursuit.

On Coruscant, Yoda called the Council to the War Room in the Temple. Ki-Adi-Mundi, Clone Commander Cody and Aayla Secura all appeared via holograms. Commander Cody reported that Obi-Wan had made contact with General Grievous and that clone troops were attacking droid troops on Utapau.

Mace Windu ordered Anakin to deliver the news to the Chancellor in order that they might gauge his intentions from his reaction.

Anakin obeyed and left the room as the holograms faded.

As soon as he'd gone Ki-Adi-Mundi and Yoda reappeared to continue talking with Mace.

"I sense a plot to destroy the Jedi. The dark side of the Force surrounds the Chancellor," warned Mace.

Ki-Adi-Mundi added: "If he does not give up his emergency powers after the destruction of Grievous, then he should be removed from office."

"The Jedi Council would have to take control of the Senate to secure a peaceful transition," said Mace. "To a dark place this line of thought will carry us. Great care, we must take," said Yoda.

Anakin went straight from the War Room to the Chancellor's office to bring him the news that Obi-Wan had engaged General Grievous.

"We can only hope Master Kenobi is up to the challenge," Palpatine said.

"I should be with him," Anakin said.

The Chancellor shook his head. "The Council doesn't seem to appreciate your talents," he told Anakin. "Don't you wonder why they won't make you a Jedi Master?"

Anakin shrugged, answering that he felt increasingly excluded. "I know there are things about the Force they're not telling me," he moaned.

It was time for Palpatine to be frank. "They don't trust you, Anakin," he said. "They see your future and know your power will be too strong to control. You must break through the fog of lies. Let me help you to know the subtleties of the Force."

Anakin stared at him in surprise. What could this ageing politician know of the Force?

"My mentor taught me everything about the Force, even the nature of the dark side," Palpatine said. "If one is to understand the great mystery, one must study all its aspects, not just the dogmatic, narrow view of the Jedi.

"If you wish to become a wise leader, you must embrace a wider view of the Force. Only through me can you achieve a power greater than any Jedi. Learn to know the dark side and you'll be able to save your wife from certain death."

Anakin's eyes blazed. He ignited his lightsaber. "You're the Sith Lord!"

Palpatine's tone was urgent. "Listen to me. Don't continue to be a pawn of the Jedi Council.

Ever since I've known you, you've been searching for a life greater than that of an ordinary Jedi. A life of significance."

Palpatine turned his back on the angry Jedi Knight. "Are you going to kill me?" he asked.

"I'd like to," replied Anakin.

Palpatine seemed pleased. "I know. I can feel your anger. It gives you focus, makes you stronger."

Anakin switched off his lightsaber and said he would turn the Chancellor over to the Council.

"Know the power of the dark side, Anakin," called Palpatine. "It's the power to save Padmé."

On Utapau, Obi-Wan and General Grievous were involved in a death-defying chase through the tunnels beneath the city.

Catching up with his foe, Obi-Wan grabbed the

droid leader's electronic staff. Obi-Wan tried to yank it away and use it to stop Grievous's wheel bike but the General pulled back and hauled Obi-Wan off the lizard, accidentally pulling him onto the bike.

Grievous reached for his pistol and tried shooting Obi-Wan behind him. But they both had to jump as the bike reached the edge of a cliff.

Now reduced to hand-to-hand combat Obi-Wan struggled to avoid the deadly blows of the brutal droid leader. But he spotted a weakness.

As the General rammed Obi-Wan's hand into a metal wall, almost breaking it, the Jedi noticed Grievous's stomach plate was loose. Obi-Wan ripped it off, revealing the alien life form's guts encased in a bag within the cyborg's chest.

Roaring with anger, Grievous kicked Obi-Wan over and tossed him off the edge of the landing platform. Obi-Wan desperately hung on.

Grievous grabbed his staff and charged, but at the last second Obi-Wan used the Force to retrieve Grievous's laser pistol, simultaneously leaping back up onto safe ground.

He blasted Grievous several times in his exposed stomach area and the alien exploded from the inside out.

"So uncivilized," muttered Obi-Wan, as he walked past the carcass to his starfighter.

Meanwhile, Anakin caught up with Mace Windu in a hangar. He and three other Jedi Knights were on their way to tell the Chancellor that Obi-Wan had destroyed General Grievous and ensure Palpatine returned his emergency powers to the Senate.

"He won't give up his power. I've just learned the terrible truth. I think Palpatine is a Sith Lord," said Anakin.

Mace was incredulous. "How do you know this?" he asked.

"He knows the ways of the Force and has been trained to use the dark side," Anakin said.

"Then our worst fears have been realised," Mace said. "We must move quickly if the Jedi Order is to survive."

Anakin offered to help arrest Palpatine, but Mace declined.

"Fear clouds your judgement," he said. "If what you told me is true, you will have gained my trust, but for now remain in the Council Chamber until we return."

That night, Anakin remained in the Council Chamber. While he sat thinking of Padmé he heard Palpatine's voice clearly.

"You do know, don't you," it reminded him, "that if the Jedi destroy me, any chance of saving Padmé will be lost."

Tears ran down Anakin's cheeks as he weighed the odds of the two paths his life could take from this point on. Making up his mind, he rushed out of the Chamber to his speeder and set off towards the Senate Office Building.

Mace Windu, Agen Kolar, Kit Fisto and Saesee Tiin entered the Chancellor's office.

Mace wasted no time. "In the name of the Galactic Senate of the Republic you are under arrest, Chancellor," he said. All four Jedi ignited their lightsabers.

"Are you threatening me?" growled Palpatine.

"The Senate will decide your fate," Mace responded.

"I am the Senate," raged Palpatine.

"Not yet!" exclaimed Mace. But before he could step forward, the Chancellor pulled a lightsaber out of his cloak sleeve and span towards them in the air. Within seconds three Jedi were no more.

Palpatine and Mace fought tooth and nail down the hallway and into a reception room.

Their lightsabers locked and they fell towards the window which smashed. Wind whipped the two figures on the sill but still neither stepped down until Palpatine tired and Mace kicked him to the floor.

Anakin arrived to find the Sith Lord pinned to the ground by Mace's lightsaber.

"Anakin!" Palpatine croaked. "I was right. The Jedi are taking over."

"The oppression of the Sith will never return," shouted Mace.

"No! No! No! You will die," screamed Palpatine, raising his hands. Lightning bolts shot out of both palms. Mace blocked them with his lightsaber.

Anakin didn't know what to do. His mentor the

politician and the respected Jedi Master both claimed the other was the traitor.

"I have the power to save the one you love," cried Palpatine. "You must choose."

"Don't listen to him," cried Mace.

Palpatine's face changed before Anakin's eyes. As Mace pushed his lightsaber closer to Palpatine, the bolts from Palpatine's hands began to arch back onto the Chancellor and his face began to twist and distort. His skin puckered and his eyes yellowed as he struggled to intensify his powers.

"Don't let him kill me," he croaked. "Anakin, help me. I can't hold on any longer."

Mace pushed his saber towards the Chancellor.

"I'm going to end this once and for all," he said.

"You can't. He must stand trial," cried Anakin. Mace told Anakin Palpatine was too dangerous to be left alive.

"It's not the Jedi way. He must live," Anakin cried. As Mace raised his lightsaber to kill the Chancellor, Anakin let out a cry. He stepped in, cutting off Mace's lightsaber-wielding hand.

Mace screamed and Palpatine sprang to life. He hit Mace square in the chest with his powerful bolts and sent him plunging from the window ledge to his death.

Anakin sank to his knees in horror, Palpatine's evil cackles ringing in his ears. "What have I done?" he

muttered, looking into Palpatine's deformed face.

"You are fulfilling your destiny," said Palpatine. "Become my apprentice. Learn the dark side of the Force.

"I will do whatever you ask," Anakin panted. "Just help me save Padmé's life. I can't live without her."

Anakin knelt before Palpatine, pledging himself to the Sith's teaching.

Palpatine promised he'd teach him to cheat death. "A powerful Sith you will become," he roared. "Henceforth, you shall be known as Darth...Vader."

On Kashyyyk, Yoda felt a disturbance in the Force. Something truly terrible had happened.

Darth Sidious swung his dark cloak around his shoulders. "When the Jedi learn what has transpired here, they will kill us, along with all the Senators," he told Anakin.

"Every single Jedi, including your friend Kenobi, is now an enemy of the Republic."

Anakin nodded. "I understand, Master," he said.

Then Sidious gave his first orders to his new Sith, Darth Vader. "We must move quickly to destroy the Jedi and prevent eternal civil war. First go to the Jedi Temple. Show no mercy. Only then will you be strong enough with the dark side to save Padmé."

Anakin could think of nothing but saving his love. "What about the other Jedi across the galaxy?" he asked.

"They will be dealt with," said Palpatine. "After you've killed all the Jedi in the Temple, go to the Mustafar system. Wipe out Viceroy Gunray and the other Separatist leaders. Once more the Sith will rule the galaxy, and we shall have peace."

As Anakin headed for the Temple with a battalion of clone troopers, the Jedi Knights scattered across the galaxy had no idea what was about to occur.

"The time has come. Execute Order 66," Darth Sidious told the clones he'd already enlisted to his side.

Obi-Wan had just finished chatting with Commander Cody and was racing across the battlefield cutting down droids when a volley of laser blasts knocked him and his lizard off the wall.

Before he plummeted down into the water-filled sink hole, he just had time to look back and see that his ally Cody and his own clone troops had fired on him.

Ki-Adi-Mundi was busy deflecting enemy fire, supported by clone troops on the crystal planet of Mygeeto. Suddenly the clones stopped behind him. The Jedi turned to see what was wrong and was killed instantly by their fire.

In the forest of Felucia, Aayla Secura and her clone troops braced themselves for an ambush by the droid army. One trooper took a message from Sidious and without warning, the clones blasted Aayla in the back, firing on her until she lay dead.

In the skies of Cato Neimoidia, Plo Koon headed his ship towards battle but the four clone pilots with him suddenly dropped back and blasted him out of the sky.
The same happened to Stass Allie on her speeder bike on Saleucami. She crashed in a huge explosion when hit by her former clone allies.

On Kashykk, Yoda watched as Commander Gree approached with one officer. When they were almost upon him they revealed their weapons, but Yoda was prepared. He knew the Force had irrevocably shifted. Pulling out his lightsaber he beheaded both clones. Chewbacca, the Wookiee, called out to him and silently Yoda leapt up onto the creature's furry back to escape.

In the Jedi Temple, Anakin entered a room full of younglings. They were huddled in a corner. "Master Skywalker," said one, his high voice trembling with fear. "There are too many of them. What should we do?"
Anakin stared at the child with blank eyes and wordlessly drew his lightsaber.

Across the city Padmé burst into tears as she looked out of her window and saw flames from the burning Temple.

Senator Bail Organa had also seen the plumes of smoke billowing from the Temple. He raced there on his speeder and found four clone troopers guarding the entrance.

"What's going on here?" he asked.

"There's been a rebellion sir, don't worry, the situation is under control," said the clone sergeant, turning Bail away. "It's time for you to leave."

"So it is," said Bail, leaping back towards his speeder and taking cover in time to see Zett Jukassa, a young Padawan, run on to the landing platform, swinging his lightsaber at clone troopers and felling

several. He was almost at Bail's speeder when Commander Appo shot him dead.

"No!" screamed Bail, horrified. Unable to believe his own eyes, he leapt into his speeder and raced away, the clone's blasts ringing through the air behind him.

In the hills overlooking the lake on Kashyyyk, Yoda bade farewell to his Wookiee friends.

"Goodbye Tarfful. Goodbye Chewbacca. Miss you, I will." The Wookiees growled their farewell and Yoda climbed into an escape pod.

Obi-Wan swam through underwater caves to the surface of Utapau. He removed his breathing apparatus and clipped it back on his utility belt.

Slowly he began to climb the steep rock side of the sink hole. He waited for the clone troopers searching for his body to give up, then made his way to the starfighter on General Grievous's landing platform.

As he eased the craft into space he made contact with his friends. Bail Organa's fuzzy hologram image came into focus. "Senator Organa!" said Obi-Wan. "My clone troops turned on me, I need help."

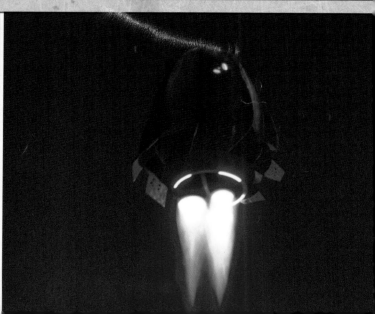

The reply was unsettling. "We have just rescued master Yoda," said Bail. "It appears this ambush has happened everywhere. We're sending you our co-ordinates."

At the same time, back on Coruscant Anakin came home. Padmé rushed onto the Veranda as she saw his starfighter dock.

"Are you alright? "she cried, embracing Anakin. "I heard there was an attack on the Jedi Temple. You can see the smoke from here."

"I'm fine," Anakin told her. "I came to see if you and the baby are safe."

"What's happening?" asked Padmé, her face a mixture of fear and sadness.

Anakin told her that the Jedi had tried to overthrow the Republic. She refused to believe it.

"I saw Master Windu attempt to assassinate the Chancellor myself," Anakin said, walking inside, away from her searching gaze.

"I will not betray the Republic," he told her carefully. "My loyalties lie with the Chancellor and with the Senate – and with you."

"What about Obi-Wan?" she asked.

"We can only hope he's remained loyal to the Chancellor," he said, taking Padmé into his arms.

"Have faith, my love," he cooed. "The Chancellor has given me a very important mission. The Separatists have gathered on Mustafar. I'm going there to end this war. Wait for me. Things will be different, I promise."

Kissing her once more, he headed back to his starfighter and sped away.

Deep in space Obi-Wan's ship docked inside Bail Organa's starcruiser and the heroes regrouped.

"How many Jedi managed to survive?" Obi-Wan asked. Yoda told him that they'd heard from no one else and Bail added that he'd seen thousands of troops attack the Temple.

Yoda told Obi-Wan they'd received a coded retreat message from the Temple requesting all Jedi to return there because the war was over.

Obi-Wan's answer was characteristically brave. "We must go back! If there are any stragglers, they'll fall into the trap," he said. The trio and two pilots headed towards Coruscant.

As they flew they received another message. This time from Senator Mas Amedda, Palpatine's aide, saying the Chancellor requested Yoda's presence at a special session of congress.

"Could be a trap," warned Bail.

"I don't think so," said Obi-Wan. "The Chancellor will not be able to control the thousands of star systems without keeping the Senate intact."

Yoda agreed. "If a special session of Congress there is, easier for us to enter the Jedi Temple, it will be."

As the Jedi landed on Coruscant, Anakin arrived in Mustafar. He pulled up his hood and strode menacingly into the control centre.

The Separatists had been told by Darth Sidious, that his new apprentice would look after them.

"Welcome, Lord Vader. We've been expecting you," said Nute Gunray.

Anakin said nothing. He raised one hand towards a control panel and closed all exits using the Force. The new Darth Vader then used his lightsaber to kill every one of the Separatist leaders.

The special session of Congress was in progress on Coruscant. Bail Organa arrived just in time to hear Palpatine's speech about the supposed Jedi plot to overthrow the Senate.

"The remaining Jedi will be hunted down and defeated," he cried. "The attempt on my life has left me scarred and deformed, but I assure you, my resolve has never been stronger."

There was thunderous applause.

"In order to ensure continuing stability, the Republic will be reorganised into the first Galactic Empire, for a safe and secure society," Chancellor Palpatine cried.
He raised his hands, soaking up the cheers.

"So this is how liberty dies. With thunderous applause," said Padmé.

Liberty was not the only dead thing facing the Jedi. In the Temple Obi-Wan and Yoda surveyed piles of corpses, some were clones, the majority Jedi.
They walked through the ruins until they found the bodies of students.

"Not even the younglings survived," said Obi-Wan.

"Killed, not by clones, this Padawan. But by a lightsaber," Yoda said, checking a Padawan's wounds.

Obi-Wan looked at Yoda in horror. "Who?" he stuttered. "Who could have done this?" They checked the security recordings.

"It can't be… It can't be…" gasped Obi-Wan

surveying the hologram of Anakin slaughtering Jedi, including the younglings, then kneeling before Sidious to receive his title – Lord Vader.

Tears welled up Obi-Wan's eyes and he shut off the hologram.

"Destroy the Sith, we must," urged Yoda.

"Send me to kill the Emperor. I will not kill Anakin," said Obi-Wan.

"Twisted by the dark side, young Skywalker has become," said Yoda. "The boy you trained, gone he is. Use your feelings Obi-Wan and you will find him."

First Obi-Wan tried Padmé's apartment. She told him she'd last seen Anakin the day before and claimed to know nothing more.

"I need your help," Obi-Wan told her. "He's in grave danger… from himself." He paused before telling her the awful truth.

"Padmé, Anakin has turned to the dark side."

She refused to believe it, not even when he told her he'd seen a security hologram of Anakin killing younglings, nor when he explained that Anakin had been deceived by Palpatine, in reality a Sith Lord.

"You're going to kill him, aren't you?" she asked.

"He has become a very great threat," Obi-Wan replied. He turned to face her. "Anakin is the father, isn't he?" he asked, looking at her swollen stomach.

Padmé looked away. "I'm so sorry," said Obi-Wan turning towards his craft.

As soon as Obi-Wan left, Padmé called on Captain Typho and C-3PO and took a speeder to her nearest landing platform. Captain Typho offered his services but Padmé declined.

"There is no danger," she said. "The fighting is over and this is personal. Besides," she added, "Threepio will look after me."

Typho bowed and returned to the city on the speeder while Padmé and C-3PO boarded a Naboo Skiff.

"I think I'm beginning to get the hang of this flying business," chattered the droid, taking off. Padmé sobbed.

Darth Vader and Sidious were in contact via hologram. "The Separatists have been taken care of, my Master," said Vader.

"It is finished then," smiled Sidious. "Send a message to the ships of the Trade Federation. All droid units must shut down immediately."

"Very good My Lord," said Vader, seeing Padmé's ship arriving on screen. He strode out to meet her.

Seeing Anakin run up to the Skiff, Padmé rushed out. The pair embraced – simply two people in love.

"What are you doing out here?" asked Anakin.

"I was so worried. Obi-Wan told me terrible things," she said. "He said you have turned to the dark side, that you killed younglings."

Anakin looked away. "Obi-Wan is trying to turn you against me," he said.

"He cares about us. He knows and wants to help you," she cried. "Anakin, all I want is your love."

Anakin stared grimly at her. "Love won't save you Padmé. Only my new powers can do that."

She shook her head. "You're a good person. Don't do this."

He was fierce now. "I won't lose you the way I lost my mother. I'm becoming more powerful than any Jedi and I'm doing it to protect you."

Padmé was crying again. "Come away with me to raise our child," she pleaded.

"Don't you see," he laughed. "We don't have to run away any more. I have brought peace to the Republic. I am more powerful than the Chancellor. I can overthrow him and you and I can rule the galaxy. Make things as we want them to be."

Padmé backed away. "Obi-Wan was right," she gasped. "You've changed."

The mere mention of his former master enraged Anakin now. "The Jedi turned against me," he cried. "Don't you turn against me."

"Anakin, you're breaking my heart," Padmé sobbed. "You're going down a path I can't follow."

But Anakin was blinded by jealousy. "Because of Obi-Wan?" he screeched.

"No. Because of what you've done, what you plan to do. Stop now. Come back. I love you," she implored.

Obi-Wan, who had stowed away on Padmé's Skiff, appeared in the doorway of the craft. Convinced she'd brought Obi-Wan to kill him, Anakin began to strangle Padmé. She crumpled to the ground, unconscious.

"You turned her against me!" Anakin screamed at Obi-Wan.

"You've done that yourself," Obi-Wan replied.

"You will not take her from me," cried the former Jedi turned Sith, flinging off his cloak.

"Your anger and lust for power have already done that," said Obi-Wan. He too, flung off his cloak. The pair circled each other like gladiators.

"Don't lecture me, I see through the lies of the Jedi," said Anakin. "I do not fear the dark side as you do. I have brought peace, freedom and justice to my new Empire." Anakin continued.

"Your new Empire?" cried Obi-Wan.

Anakin's eyes glowed yellow in the dark. "Don't make me kill you," he screeched. "If you're not with me then you're my enemy."

"Only a Sith deals in absolutes," cried Obi-Wan. "I will do what I must."

"You will try," said Anakin igniting his lightsaber.

Obi-Wan's lightsaber also hummed to life. And so began the most ferocious of fights. The Jedi and the Sith had spent so long together that each could anticipate the other's next move. They both used every jump, leap and trick

in the book and consistently blocked and parried the other's blows in endless combat.

On Coruscant, Yoda entered the Chancellor's office. He used the Force to throw two guards against the wall, knocking them out.

"I hear a new apprentice you have, Emperor," said Yoda to the figure in the chair. "Or should I call you, Darth Sidious?"

"Master Yoda, you survived," said Sidious, raising one eyebrow. "Your arrogance blinds you," he continued. "Now you will experience the full power of the dark side."

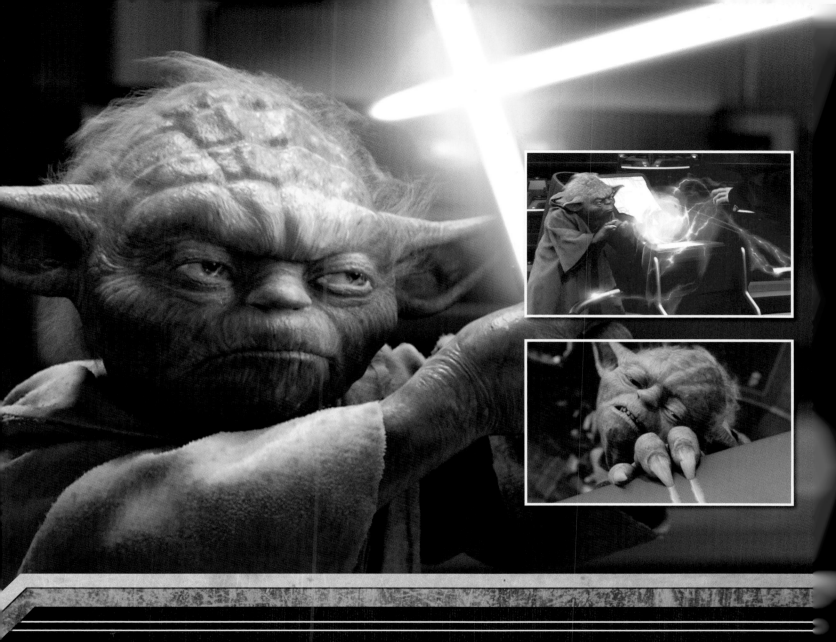

The Dark Lord raised his arms and Force lightning shot out of his palms, throwing Yoda across the room.

"I have waited a long time for this moment, my little green friend," he cackled. "At last, the Jedi are no more."

Yoda opened one eye. "Not if anything to say about it, I have," he said, using the power of the Force to throw Darth Sidious over his desk.

"At an end your rule is and not short enough it was," he said. Darth Sidious flew through the air towards the exit. Yoda stopped him.

"If so powerful you are, why leave?" he asked, igniting his lightsaber.

"You will not stop me. Darth Vader will become more powerful than either of us," rasped Sidious, igniting his lightsaber.

"Faith in your new apprentice and in the dark side, misplaced are," said Yoda.

The blades collided in fast and furious combat. The fight moved to the vast Senate Chamber. Sidious got into the Chancellor's podium pod, which began to rise into the arena. Yoda made a giant leap in with him.

When close combat became unproductive, Yoda jumped to a lower pod. Sidious used the Force to hurl pod after pod at Yoda who ducked and jumped between flying pods to avoid getting hit.

As the tiny Jedi leapt around, Sidious turned and aimed deadly lightning at him. It caught the Jedi Master mid-air and threw him back, disarming him. Without his weapon, Yoda had no choice but to retreat.

Yoda squeezed himself into a small wiring chute and crawled along, gasping a mayday into his comlink.

"Activate your homing beacon when you're ready," said Bail Organa's voice from his speeder.

"Hurry, careful timing we will need, said Yoda."

Floating down to floor-level in his pod, Sidious confronted his guards who admitted they hadn't yet found a body.

"Then he's not dead," yelled the Sith. "Double your search." He paused for a moment and stiffened, sensing something.

"Prepare my shuttle for immediate take-off," he told Mas Amedda. "Lord Vader is in danger."

As Darth Sidious sped off in the direction of Mustafar, a lone speeder hovered by an outlet pipe at the back of the Senate building. Yoda climbed out to find Bail Organa waiting for him.

He climbed into the passenger seat of the speeder and Bail gunned the engines. Yoda seemed to have shrunk into himself slightly. His shoulders slumped.

"Into exile I must go," he told his loyal friend. "Failed, I have."

Bail said nothing, but flew the disenchanted Jedi Master into the heavy city traffic.

On Mustafar, Obi-Wan and Anakin's fight had intensified. They'd moved from the landing pad to the control centre and now found themselves on top of a pipe spanning a lava river. They worked their way to the middle, fighting ferociously, each trying to push the other to a fiery end. Reaching the other side they moved to a huge metal structure made up of platforms over the river.

They jumped from one to the other until a huge spray of lava began to melt the frame. Support for the entire structure fell away and it fell, with the Jedi and Sith clinging on to the tallest tower, into the lava river.

They continued to fight climbing to the highest point as the tower melted beneath them, sinking under the lava.

Obi-Wan grabbed an overhanging cable and leapt from the tower. Anakin did the same, and the pair continued their lightsaber fight as they swung past each other.

Knowing he could only hold on for so long, Obi-Wan back-flipped down onto a floating platform in the middle of the raging torrent of lava. Anakin landed on a worker droid which had fallen in, too. Still the battle raged.

"I have failed you, Anakin," Obi-Wan called above the roar of the lava falls. "Chancellor Palpatine, is evil," he said.

"From my point of view, the Jedi are evil," Anakin answered.

"Well then you truly are lost," said Obi-Wan.

Anakin flipped onto Obi-Wan's platform and swung his lightsaber.

But seeing his chance Obi-Wan jumped towards safety on the black sandy bank.

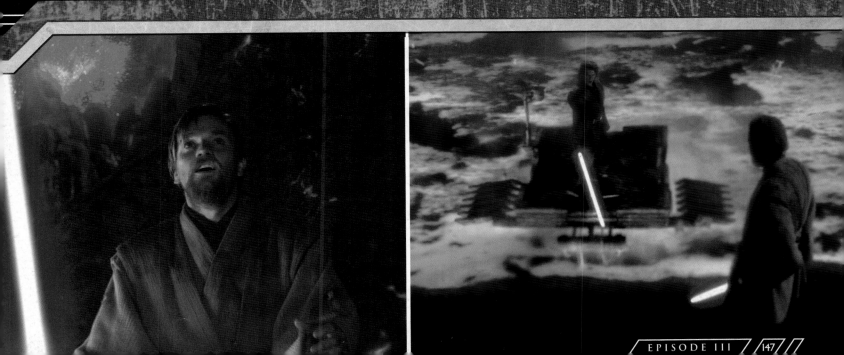

"It's over, Anakin," yelled Obi-Wan.

"You underestimate my power!" replied Anakin.

Obi-Wan tried to warn his former apprentice against pursuing an attack on the river bank, but Anakin was consumed by the wish for revenge.

He jumped onto the bank, landing in the sand a few feet below Obi-Wan. While he regained his balance Obi-Wan whirled his lightsaber. With one blow he severed Anakin's legs at the knees and his good arm at the shoulder.

Anakin let out a bloodcurdling cry. He tumbled down the embankment and rolled to the edge of the lava. He used his remaining mechanical hand to hang on to the embankment.

"You were the Chosen One!" Obi Wan cried. "It was said you would destroy the Sith, not join them. Bring balance to the Force, not leave it in darkness."

He picked up Anakin's lightsaber and began to walk away.

"I hate you!" screamed Anakin.

"You were my brother, Anakin," cried Obi-Wan, turning back to see the awful sight on the bank. "I loved you."

The Jedi wept as Anakin's clothing blew into the lava river and caught fire. In seconds his former apprentice was engulfed by flames.

As Obi-Wan reached Padmé's skiff he spotted C-3PO. "Master Kenobi," said the droid. "We have Miss Padmé on board. Please hurry. We should leave this dreadful place."

Inside, Padmé opened her eyes for one second. "Obi-Wan?" she pleaded. "Is Anakin alright?"

Obi-Wan brushed a strand of hair from Padmé's face. She lost consciousness before he was forced to answer.

Not long after the skiff had left, an Imperial shuttle closed its wings and settled on the highest of the landing platforms on Mustafar.

A platoon of clone troopers emerged, followed by Darth Sidious. The Dark Lord walked in front of the marching clones to the volcanic pit where he discovered Anakin's remains.

"There he is, your Majesty," said the Clone Commander.

"He's still alive," said Sidious.

Anakin groaned and flipped over on the sand, displaying his grotesquely burnt face.

"Get a medical capsule, immediately," Sidious ordered.

Sidious flew Anakin back to the Imperial Rehab Centre on Coruscant. Anakin's body was carried inside in a floating medical capsule.

Meanwhile, in another medical facility on Polis Massa, medical droids were working on a bizarre case.

"Medically, she is completely healthy," a droid told Obi-Wan and Bail Organa as they looked at Padmé in her hospital bed. "But for reasons we can't explain, we are losing her."

"She's dying?" Obi-Wan asked.

"We don't know why," said the droid. "She has lost the will to live. We need to operate quickly if we are to save the babies."

"Babies?" cried an astonished Bail.

"She's carrying twins," the droid confirmed.

Yoda looked terribly sad at hearing this news.

Obi-Wan walked to the window and placed his hand over his mouth in shock and grief.

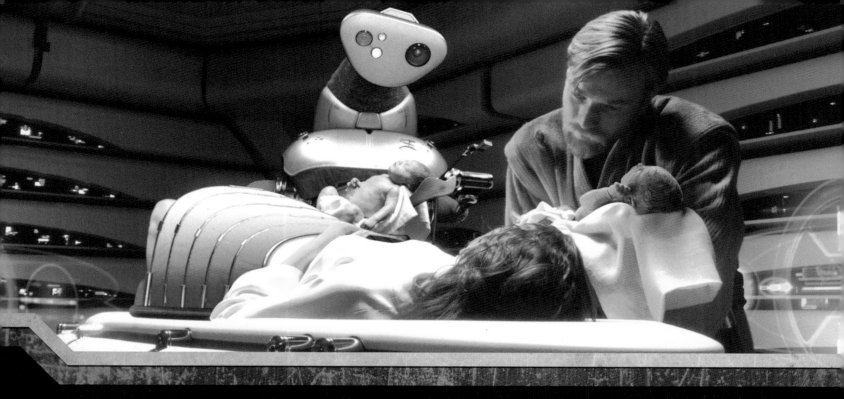

That night two new lives sparked on Polis Massa.

"It's a boy," the medical droid told Obi-Wan as it delivered the baby from Padmé's body. Heavily sedated, she still winced from the pain.

Obi-Wan took the boy in his arms and showed him to Padmé.

"Oh Luke," she breathed, smiling faintly.

"Push, push," urged the droid. Padmé cried out and soon her cries were joined by the cries of the second twin.

"And a girl…"said the droid.

"It's a girl," Obi-Wan repeated.

"Leia," said Padmé.

Obi-Wan leant over Padmé, speaking softly to her. Suddenly Padmé seemed to find the strength to speak. "Obi-Wan," she began. "There is good in him. I know…I know…there…is…still…"

And with those words, the ultimate expression of faith in and love for Anakin, Senator Padmé Amidala passed away.

Yoda, watching from the doorway, looked away in sorrow.

In the Imperial Rehab Centre a different kind of birth was taking place. Droids had operated for hours on the remains of Anakin Skywalker.

His missing legs and arm had been replaced with

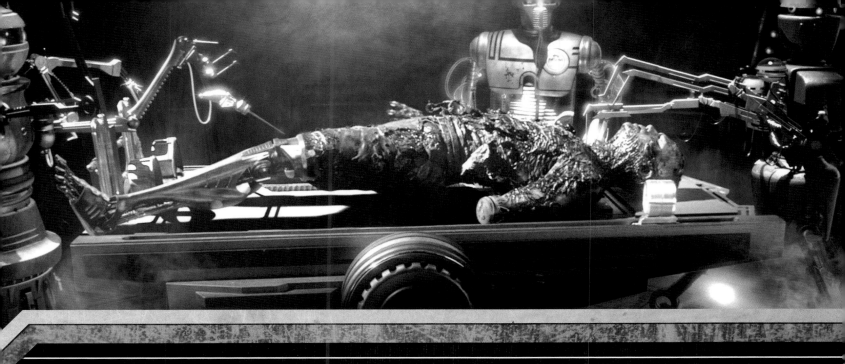

shiny new, robotic limbs and the rest of his torso was clad in black body armour, complete with built in life-support.

Anakin moaned and cried out as the droids prodded, poked and injected him, but at last he lay still on the table. He stared up to see a black mask, dropping towards his face from above. The droids fitted a helmet over it and with a hiss it sealed tight. Darth Vader began breathing.

Suddenly the operating table slid upright. Darth Sidious crossed the floor to stand beside his creation.

"Lord Vader, can you hear me?" he asked.

"Yes, Master," crackled Vader, each breath a rasp. He looked at Sidious.

"Where is Padmé? Is she safe?" he asked. "Is she alright?"

There was a pause. "It seems in your anger you killed her," Sidious lied.

A low groan emanated from Vader's mask. "I, I couldn't have! She was alive. I felt it," he moaned, anger fuelling the darkness in him.

Darth Sidious smiled evilly. He knew he had broken what little remained of Anakin's spirit.

In a fury of bitterness and pain, Vader burst out of his bonds. His screams echoed throughout the centre for a long, long time.

Somewhere else in the galaxy Bail Organa's starcruiser approached the city of Theed. Bail, Yoda and Obi-Wan sat around a conference table.

"Hidden, safe, the children must be kept," said Yoda.

"We must take them somewhere the Sith will not sense their presence," added Obi-Wan.

"Split up they should be," said Yoda.

"My wife and I will take the girl," smiled Bail. "We've always talked of adopting a baby girl. She will be loved with us."

"And what of the boy?" asked Obi-Wan. Yoda turned to him." To Tatooine. To his family, send him."

"I will take the child and watch over him, Obi-Wan promised.

"Until the time is right, disappear we will," ordered Yoda.

On his way out of the room, Yoda stopped Obi-Wan. "Master Kenobi," he said. "In your solitude on Tatooine, training I have for you."

Obi-Wan was surprised. "Training?" he asked.

"An old friend has learned the path to immortality," said Yoda enigmatically. "One who has returned from the nether world of the Force."

Seeing Obi-Wan's confusion, he explained further. "Your old Master."

"Qui-Gon?" smiled Obi-Wan delightedly.

Yoda nodded. "How to commune with him, I will teach you."

As the starcruiser reached its final destination Bail Organa spoke to the Captain.

"I'm placing these droids in your care, Captain Antilles. Treat them well. Clean them up. Have the protocol droid's mind wiped."

"Oh no," said C-3PO. R2 beeped worriedly beside him.

Meanwhile on Naboo, the people buried their former queen. Senator Padmé Amidala was given a full state funeral. Crowds lined the street to mourn as her flowered coffin, drawn by six beautiful, white beasts made its way through the city. As the tragic young woman was laid to rest anyone close enough to the casket would have seen that in her hand she clutched the Japor necklace, given to her by her true love, Anakin Skywalker.

The mother was no more, but elsewhere in the galaxy her twins began their new lives surrounded by love. Bail Organa brought Leia home to his wife, the Queen of Alderaan, while Obi-Wan Kenobi rode up to Criegg Lars' moisture farm homestead on an Eopie, a precious bundle in his arms. Carefully he handed baby Luke to Owen and Beru, Anakin's step brother and his wife. Together, the new family watched the twin suns set.

KI-ADI-MUNDI

With his enlarged conical head containing a binary brain, Ki-Adi-Mundi is a very recognisable presence on the Jedi Council. His greatest strength is also perhaps his greatest weakness, because as a skilled thinker and tactician he finds it difficult to accept things that go against his perceived wisdom – such as his disbelief that the Sith could have survived hidden for a millennia or that the former Jedi Dooku has turned to the dark side.

Born on the planet Cerea, Ki-Adi-Mundi is unusual in the ranks of the Jedi for being permitted into training after infancy. When he was already four years old a mysterious Jedi Master known only as the 'Dark Woman' arrived on Cerea, as she had heard of Ki's powerful ability to manipulate objects with his mind. She took him to the Jedi Temple where he was put into training under Yoda. Due to the low birth rate of his species, he is exempt from the proscription on Jedi forming lengthy relationships and marrying. As a result he has several wives and children (although he tries not to form too strong attachments to them).

When he realises that war against the Separatists is inevitable, he is pressed into service, becoming a General commanding the Galactic Marines. At one point he suggests the Jedi take control of the Senate, fearing Palpatine is becoming too powerful. Such talk could be considered treason, but he is determined that democracy must prevail and that the Republic must not become a dictatorship. His idea is never enacted due to Palpatine issuing Order 66, which decimates the Jedi.

DID YOU KNOW?

The main reason Ki-Adi-Mundi is permitted several wives is because there are 20 female Cereans born to every male, making each male vital to the survival of the species.

COMMANDER CODY

Like all clone troopers, Commander Cody is a genetically manipulated clone of Jango Fett. Cody is actually his nickname, as his real designation is CC-2224, which is what he is known as until the Clone Wars. During his training on Kamino, he showed a penchant for individual thought and independence, making him stand out from the other clones. As was often the case, those clones that showed special qualities quickly caught the attention of the watchful Kaminoans, who selected CC-2224 for special training.

He receives more training during the Clone Wars, which is designed to augment field commanders that show a flair for independent action. The process awakens 2224's dormant personality and soon afterwards he takes the name Cody and personal affectations begin to show up in his actions and his armour, as well his installation of a jetpack on his clone armour. He is assigned to Obi-Wan Kenobi through most of the Clone Wars, but as the Jedi is often away on special missions, it falls to Cody to lead the 7th Sky Corps and take command of the 212th Attack Battalion. Extremely skilled in tactics, he's a no-nonsense soldier who is loyal and, as his breeding ensures, always follows order. His ability for independent thought allows him to be exceptional in battle, but that doesn't mean he'll question the Republic.

Providing vital support to Kenobi in numerous battles, Cody and his troopers become a vital part of the Republic's fight against the Separatists. After the creation of the Empire, he remains in the service of the former Republic, becoming a Commander in the first wave of Imperial Stormtroopers.

DID YOU KNOW?

Even though he has worked with Kenobi for several years, he has little compunction about trying to kill his former friend when Order 66 comes through.

GENERAL GRIEVOUS

Despite his droid appearance, Grievous was born the completely organic Qymaen jai Sheelal, a member of the Kaleesh species from the planet Kalee. Skilled in the art of war, his hatred of the Jedi stems from their leaving his people to starve on their home planet, after the Order sided with the Kaleesh's enemy, the Huk.

When he has working for the Intergalactic Banking Clan, he was betrayed by a close ally and critically injured, with only his brain, part of his head and some of vital organs surviving. These few parts were then incorporated into a new, mainly droid body. In this different, largely mechanical form, he is taken under the wing of Count Dooku, who trains him in lightsaber combat – something his droid parts make him particularly adept at. Dooku knows he has a powerful force in Grievous, and pits him against powerful opponents to prove Grievous is capable of leading the droid army. With an absolutely ruthless nature, Grievous is so successful that to many he eclipses Dooku as the main threat of the Separatist movement. He essentially becomes the face of the enemy.

Grievous is a powerful and decisive part of the Separatists' fight against the Republic, but his main passion remains killing Jedi and he has a number of their deaths on his hands. After the fall of Dooku, the Jedi believe the only thing that stands in the way of peace is Grievous, and so killing or capturing him becomes their top priority.

DID YOU KNOW?

Grievous's first lightsaber belonged to Jedi Master Sifo-Dyas, the man who initially ordered the Clone Army from the Kaminoans.

DARTH VADER

Ever since he was brought to the Jedi Temple as a boy, Anakin Skywalker was thought to have a clouded future. The Jedi Council's fears prove well founded when Darth Sidious starts to take an interest in the young Jedi. The Sith Lord plays on Anakin's fears, anger and desire for power to manipulate him to the dark side of the Force. When Anakin agrees to become Sidious' new apprentice, he is renamed Darth Vader. The new Sith soon proves how ruthless and malevolent he is, by going to the Jedi Temple to kill the younglings.

Shortly afterwards, Vader is nearly killed during a battle with Obi-Wan Kenobi on the volcanic planet Mustafar. He is saved by Palpatine, and his burned, maimed body is rebuilt and placed in a black, helmeted suit, which acts as both an imposing exterior and as a life support system for the newly reborn Darth Vader.

Vader is the incredibly loyal right-hand man of the Emperor, who uses intimidation and his Force powers to control those around him. An utterly ruthless figure, Vader becomes a vicious, single-minded enforcer, dedicated to the dark side and on tightening the hold he and his Master have over the galaxy. To most he is the personification of evil that Emperor Palpatine needs to keep the population cowed. However Vader underestimates the resilience of the Rebel Alliance that opposes the Empire, as well as the feelings stirred up inside him by the emergence of a young man called Luke.

DID YOU KNOW?

Darth Vader's trademark heavy breathing is a result of the mechanical lungs needed to keep him alive, which are part of the extensive machinery hidden inside his suit.

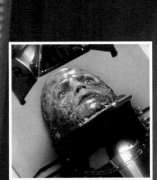

Recycling

ANGELA ROYSTON

WAYLAND

Environment Starts Here!
Recycling

OTHER TITLES IN THE SERIES
Water · Food · Transport

Produced for Wayland Publishers Limited by

Lionheart Books
10, Chelmsford Square
London NW10 3AR
England

Designer: Ben White
Editor: Lionel Bender
Picture Research: Madeleine Samuel
Electronic make-up: Mike Pilley, Radius
Illustrated by Rudi Vizi

First Published in 1998 by Wayland Publishers Limited
61 Western Road, Hove, East Sussex BN3 1JD
© Copyright 1998 Wayland Publishers Limited

Find Wayland on the internet at http://www.wayland.co.uk

British Library Cataloguing in Publication Data
Royston, Angela
Recycling. - (Environment starts here! ; 3)
1. Recycling (Waste, etc.) - Juvenile literature
I. Title
363.7'282

ISBN 0 7502 2231 X

Printed and bound by Eurografica S.p.A., Vicenza, Italy

Picture Acknowledgements
Pages 1: Ecoscene/Nick Hawkes. 4: Eye Ubiquitous/Craig Hutchins. 7: Wayland Picture
Library. 9. Ecoscene/Lorenzo Lees. 10: Ecoscene/Ian Harwood. 11: Britstock/IFA-Bernard
Ducke. 12: Eye Ubiquitous/Steve Miller. 14: Zefa/Stockmarket. 15: Ecoscene/Kevin King.
16: Zefa/Stockmarket. 17: Britstock/IFA-Hans Jurgen Wiedl. 18: Eye Ubiquitous/Jim Winkley.
19: Ecoscene/Towse. 20: Ecoscene/Sally Morgan. 21: Eye Ubiquitous/Paul Seheult. 21(inset):
Ecoscene/Sally Morgan. 22: Wayland/Angus Blackburn. 23, 24, 25, 26: Zefa/Stockmarket.
27: Ecoscene/Rob Nichol. 28: Ecoscene/Stuart Donachie. 29: Zefa/Stockmarket.
Cover: Zefa/Stockmarket.

The photo on page 1 shows children putting newspapers into a paper recycling container.